PEACEMAKERS

PEACEMAKERS

BOOK 1

YOU and ME

A JOURNEY of SERVICE

Written by Wendy Stewart

Order this book online at www.trafford.com
or email orders@trafford.com

Most Trafford titles are also available at major online book retailers.

Printed in the United States of America.

ISBN: 978-1-4269-6338-4 (sc)
ISBN: 978-1-4269-6339-1 (e)

Trafford rev. 04/16/2011

 www.trafford.com

North America & International
toll-free: 1 888 232 4444 (USA & Canada)
phone: 250 383 6864 ♦ fax: 812 355 4082

DEDICATED TO

* Hello dear Readers and Fellow Travellers*

Many thanks to all my Guardian Angels and Teachers,
Friends and Companions.
For at any given time we are both teacher and student.
Sometimes in the smallest way, we help another traveller
Shine your Light in dark places and offer a Smile
It takes Love and Compassion to understand we are all
Walking this road Together
It takes Love to reach out and give comfort
To another who maybe struggling
Shine your Light and Reach out to touch someone.

FORWARD

What secrets lay buried deep within the matrix of the Soul computer? The memories of the many roads you have travelled to discover and experience the **real** YOU?

William Shakespeare wrote, "The world is but a stage and we are merely players."

As we go about our daily lives, we encounter many emotional and physical dramas and often ask ***why me.*** We feel a deep connection to different environments and ethnic philosophies. We engage in numerous affections for people we feel we have met or known before but cannot always fathom why. Have you experienced such an encounter, but what is more important have you ever questioned, why?

SO, what memories lay hiding in your cells, waiting to be activated on this new journey?

Which costume are you wearing right now? And which stage are you acting out this present scenario?

In our lifetime we will play many parts, arriving on one stage and exiting on another. Many people will visit our stage for a brief time, enhancing our knowledge of self, or maybe reflecting a part of ourselves that we have not recognized yet. We are all great mirrors to one another. This offers us new opportunities to discover the magic that lies deep within the heart and soul of *who you really are*. As you taste and experience the smorgasbord of emotions, interactions and relationships, you will add to your soul the wisdom that is being offered and experienced in the world of duality.

Life takes on a new flavour, a vision so much more expanded than before. Our heart beats with a new tune to unravel the mystery of why we are here. Just for a moment, take time out to review what you have just read. Ponder on its possibilities and feel the energy as your heart misses a beat. What amazing potentials sit dormant in the recesses of your Soul that you still haven't accessed?

We have all watched television programs where archaeologists uncover the past and try to paste the pieces together. The Good Book, the Bible maintains that our civilisations are only ex amount of years old. That is, it starts with the time of the flood. So what happened before the flood? Was there a world that existed with a technology greater than ours? Did they use their power to control nature's forces and create their downfall?

So I ask, how long has your journey been in progress?

Because I am a curious cat by nature, with a thousand unanswered questions, my life's journey has taken me deep into discovering new understandings of myself. You could say I walked where Angels feared to tread, in search of uncovering the hidden treasures that lay within the cave of remembering. I walked the Road Less Travelled.

I do not recommend it for the faint hearted.

You will need the Sword of Truth, the Armour of Love, the Courage and Strength of a Lion and the Wit of The Fool. Also, the conscious knowledge that Guardian Angels will never leave you Alone and will Love you through your darkest hours. Many times you will question WHY you endeavoured to walk this journey. Many times you will thank your Angels for showing you the answers to questions that appear so far removed from the present life you are living. This is my story of how and why I took the journey to complete the Cycle of Cycles, through the Light and the Dark days of uncovering the Truth.

If you have read this far into this little book, congratulations.

EVENTS

CONTROL 1 CENTRE

Within the Star System called the Milky Way, which is our exquisite playground, there are seven major space stations that monitor the delicate energy balance of this Galaxy. Created on a unique spider web design, all planets play a major part in keeping the matrix and strands of communication connected in harmony within our known universe. Any disturbance or mass destruction can create a rupture in the web. Ultimately the resonance will flow throughout the galaxies and effects ALL the other star systems.

Close to the Pleiades cluster which is often referred to as the Seven Sisters in the constellation of Taurus. The Control Space Station above Alderbarren recorded an **'Intergalactic Distress'** signal. A warning sounded on the large, crystal console, as red lights flashed.

There was a great disturbance in the Force.

＊ ＊ ＊ ＊ ＊

Soel and Solenia stood close together, hand in hand on the balcony of the Central Communications Tower surveying the magical view of their world. As soul-mates they had mastered duality many eons ago during the time of Moses when he led the Chosen Ones across the desert into the new homeland.

Since that early phase of human evolution the Universe had expanded and contracted many times in accordance with the in-breath and out-breath of God and Creation.

In this new time frame these Ancient Ones had selected to be the Guardians of the Galactic Skyways, the master computer broke the silence and they hurried inside to examine the screen, trying to locate and decipher the origin of the signal and galactic location.

"The consciousness of the Genesis programme has sent out a collective prayer for assistance. Like a big **HELP** prayer. There must be massive problems for this message to register on our technology." Soel sighed and a frown creased his forehead as he read the distress signal.

"It's been a few thousand years since the last catastrophe, when we sent the deluge to refresh the land, to renew the energy and bring the land back into balance." Solenia gazed deeply into his eyes searching for understanding. "This will be the third time in recorded history that Earth has reached another critical point of termination. This young planet has so much difficulty mastering duality," Solenia punched in the co-ordinates and waited for the connection.

"Switch to the Earth Station and let's observe what's happening," requested Soel. They stood close to each other and silently observed the chaos exploding across the screen.

"Countries are fighting over boarder-lines. Egomaniac scientists who skilfully collect super funds are secretly building weapons of mass destruction. Thousands are dying or being slaughtered, under the name of ethnic cleansing. This is horrific! Tribes are still warring over long forgotten quarrels from times so long gone that they don't remember their origins." Tears streamed down her bronze face as Solenia witnessed the loss of human life and the abuse of defenceless children, women and animals. "I can't believe that I could feel so emotional about this." She quickly turned away from the screen to conceal her emotions, wiping away a tear as she struggled to collect her thoughts.

"Do you remember the excitement of **Creation** when the Ascended Masters first had this vision of a New Planet where the Earth angels would be given *free will* and all the wonderful ideas that they composed from around the Star Systems to build a safe haven?" Soel's voice bubbled as he reminisced about the Earth Genesis and drifted off into his memory bank, recalling the millennium of planning. Soul was very aware of Solenia's connection especially as they had many descendants finishing their last initiations. He felt her distress and tried to lift her spirits.

"Yes I do. The Master's collected the most positive aspects from each Planet and combined them into the programme. Scouts were sent out to each station to survey the climate, water / land ratio, and scientists juggled with the hydrogen / oxygen balance for the new form of physical bodies and plant vegetation. It was no mean task getting the equilibrium right for human life.

What functioned on other planets was not always the ultimate answer for the Blue Planet." Solenia recalled the massive scientific groundwork.

"Those were amazing days, magnetic energy floated freely and encouraged the imagination to go beyond our known boundaries, to stretch our dreams of creating a perfect world in harmony." Soel drifted back in time as a melancholy shadow crossed his aging graceful face.

"Each planet submitted their best and finest fauna and flora to be included in the new experiment. While the Masters set out to blend the vast collection and assemble the most perfect, exotic range of plants for food, pleasure and optimum health. Then just like Noah, they collected an assortment of viable animals two by two. The Earth story is not a new one, somewhere in the consciousness when Noah was advised to build the Ark and collect the animals, it struck a cord and he knew it was a truth. A Cosmic truth, from long ago." Soel took a breath and sipped the fluid in the crystal glass. Just for a brief moment they had forgotten the present situation and enjoyed looking back to the original programme of what might have been a true haven of learning and experiencing the drama of duality in a peaceful world. "For many, many years the Blue Planet location was 'TOP Secret'. The Masters from twelve galaxies assembled to bring that plan into fruition and decided to build the Blue Planet in a remote part of the Milky Way where it would be safe from the influence of the Dark Overlords. Also, to give them sufficient time to mature in the unfamiliar energy of balancing emotions, it was a new playground. Duality is a complex situation to master. We have moved through that phase of evolution and see things how they really are. For us Truth is all we know, no diversity." Soel thankful to have completed his journey through duality and yet occasionally there were brief moments when he missed the excitement and energy of passion.

"No wonder Earth people still think they are alone in the Universe or the centre of their known Universe. The Ones who govern that planet have kept the Secret of the Federation to themselves in order to rule with fear and an iron fist." Solenia quietly contemplated the ramifications of not feeling the energy of connecting and belonging to the larger galactic family. "But wasn't there an organised format to assist progressive evolution for the inhabitants to realise that the journey they had committed to would entail more than one lifetime?" Solenia enquired, looking puzzled.

"Yes, yes there was and many indigenous tribes were aware of the long term plan and practiced their knowledge. They knew their heart connection to the Earth and Sky. It is written in their Mythology but after the Flood many people believed they had been punished by the Gods. Much of the ancient recorded information was lost to the masses, they were still uneducated and couldn't read or write. Only a select few of the Wise Ones had the fore thought to protect the written scrolls of knowledge by having their documents and archives secreted away into deep, sandstone caves on high ground. You must remember the flood happened 10,000 years ago, much has come to pass since that time. It was the Mayans and the Egyptians who knew the long term project and recorded the astrological progression of the planets and the Sun in their temples on stone walls. The lithographs explained the movements of the planets and the ages of change, fore warned of the time frames of evolution but all this would have to wait for the archaeologists to discover and translate the message to mankind. Where the pyramids in Egypt told the story of the past history of their early civilization, the Mayans recorded the future progression for mankind. These monuments were built high in the mountains and their civilisation remained undiscovered to the outside world until the 18th Century. To this day the South American tribes are familiar with our visitations and acknowledge the ancient landmarks engraved in the topography which was left by our space brothers but the governments and churches that rule still try to keep this information secret." Soel paused and returned to the screen to make further analysis, scanning the turbulent pictures.

"We will have to call for volunteers. Link up to the Galactic Federation; they all need to observe this most recent report and become involved with major decisions. It will take more than a handful of wise ones to change the energy and move forward the Blue Planet into the future program, and save the inhabitants from themselves," Soel made an executive choice and pushed the 'blue' button. This immediate concern was far too complex.

A calm, modulated female voice from the central computer announced, "Attention!" A flashing light quickly connected the out going communication on six screens. "Please wait for a communication link up. Processing now!"

The conference proceeded in a very serious tone. After calculating the number of residences, the percentage of clean up from toxic waste, the necessary amount of spiritual growth and change needed to take place within the preceding 50 years, the Council arrived at a firm conclusion and announced.

"By our present calculations, we require to assemble 144,000 mature souls who are willing to take up this great challenge, to turn this planet Earth around, to come out of the Dark and bring into the Light. These Earth inhabitants must reach a point of responsibility for their actions, environment and growth to become evolved human beings.

At present they have lost their way, like many empires through the ages, they have fallen into the *'ego'* of power and greed. Yet they have so much to offer our universe. We watch their stamina and strength through adversary. The caring for the community, the love of family, their compassion towards the infirmed and sick, but the Overlords who hold the purse strings unequivocally complicated their ability for positive spiritual growth by withholding the Truth."

"These residents of Earth have reflected much wisdom to us." After much deliberation, the 'MASTERS' announced, "We have no alternative".....

WE WILL SEND THE PIONEERS -
THE PEACEMAKERS.

"These will be the Earth Angels who have already completed many lifetimes mastering their physical, emotional, mental and spiritual aspects. We will arrange a celebration gathering and observe if we can muster the calculated numbers."

Soel and Solenia received a *'special notice'* on their computer screen, to invite the initiates from around the Galaxy to assemble on the 29th day of the second month, at the Rose Bowl, Crystal Dome.

"How many do you think will show up? I remember that many were destined to start a new program in another part of the Universe, an upgraded Genesis. These Initiates were extremely excited because it was about establishing the balance of duality, where the emotional trappings were not going to colour their judgments. And unconditional love will guide their decision-making. You know, that old thought pattern that rules "FOR THE GREATER GOOD OF ALL." reflected Solenia.

"Well this emergency is critical and I am sure *'the peacemakers'* will understand that this mission must be completed before we, as a collective, can move forward into the next stage of evolution." Soel declared matter-of-factly.

"You are right! As each point of balance is completed every soul benefits and expands. Each assists the others no matter where they are in the universal plan and that is for the greater good of all." Solenia consoled herself with compassion.

"Pull up the Solar Matrix and we will send out the invitations to those who qualify for this ominous journey and type out the SOS message on the plasma screen in Central Square."

"Well we have been given a date, now we will have to prepare for catering. What type of refreshments shall we serve?" Solenia inquired looking vaguely at Soel. "That's a huge gathering to prepare for!"

"I know. Awesome! We've never had to cater for so many at one sitting." Soel went into deep thought. Five minutes later he came up with a brilliant idea. "Well, as these volunteers are returning to Earth let's give them a special treat. As of yet, they have not experienced the fad of the future, so we will prepare a new traditional barbecue!"

"A barbecue!" exclaimed Solenia.

"Yes! A Celestial Barbecue! But we need more information, dear one."

Soel returned to his keyboard and designed a most tantalising menu. Pressed **send** to the Preparation Complex. "That will give them something to think about."

"Now we must find a way of convincing these volunteers that they are very much needed on this rescue expedition. Go into the data bank, to find the most beautiful of Natures sights and we will put together a glossy brochure. You know, azure blue lagoon waters, ancient luscious forests with weeping ferns and tall trees. And the wonderful array of wild life forms.... And include the Seven Wonders of the World because these are sacred sites where many Initiations took place in Earth history and these visions will send a message to their soul memories." Solenia became very excited as she viewed her own memory bank.

"Yeah! Okay, let's see what we can find. Computer please search for the finest natural creations on planet Earth"

Soel became engrossed in the files and scanned the program for the most superb photo graphics. Within a few hours he had assembled the majority of alluring pictures that still to this day took his breath away. Tears weld in his eyes, as he observed the full spectrum of colours and textures of the Earth planet.

"Can you believe how beautiful this planet is?" He quickly wiped the teardrop from his cheek and returned to the task in hand. "Computer SAVE." Soel turned back to Soleina with a request. "Solenia, what else can be included in this brochure? It must be enticing, almost irresistible."

"Well there's sex, and relationships… you know plenty of drama!" Her violet eyes twinkled with a wicked smiled.

"Yes, you're right. What about music and art? And the new technology?" Soel surveyed her face for approval.

"Yeah! That all sounds great." They quickly went to work assembling an incredibly tantalizing prospectus. This was serious business. Soels fingers flew across the keyboard, scanning the data. Solenia moved away to give him space to explore his imagination and made herself a refreshing fruit juice. Some hours later she returned to view his progress.

"How's it going?" Soel flashed the finished product at Solina, proud of the quality. "Great! Nice colours. That will pull them in for sure."

2

SUSTENANCE PREPARATION COMPLEX

(Known to us as the Kitchen)
URGENT MEMO

"Well, I don't know what this is all about and it doesn't give us much time to prepare for so many visitors." Omha moaned, scratched his nose and let out a deep sigh. The crimson beret that perched precariously on his pointed head only stopped falling over his eye brows, because of his large pixie ears. Although he enjoyed being master of his own domain he certainly didn't appreciate sudden changes to his already busy daily schedule.

"Tell me about it!" Cherry commented while drying her hands under the hot air from the machine on the wall. Her beautiful round, radiant face appeared concerned as an impetuous lock of white hair escaped from under her spotted scarf. "So many different cultures to cater for, how are we going to keep them all happy?"

They had worked together as partners for eons, happy in their profession as caterers to the masses but this request was definitely a first and would definitely test their professional skills.

Just the sheer numbers became a nightmare. Omha sauntered across the kitchen to where Cherry leaned heavily on the massive glass preparation bench and rapped his long arms around her ample waistline giving her a warm embrace and planted a soft kiss on her cheek and murmured in her ear. "Soel has requested a barbecue but I have no idea how we can accommodate. I need more information before I can agree to continue with his plans. I suspect we will have to come up with our own brilliant ideas from somewhere. Don't you worry my sweet?" Omha untangled himself from their discreet clinch and walked away shaking his head. His beret slipped over his left ear and fell gracefully on the polished floor.

"Well everyone's so busy attending to every day arrangements, how will we fit it all this extra work in? All they told us was that there would be 144,000 attending. What a headache," Cherry mumbled under her breath tactfully, hoping for an enlightened response.

"Yes that's true but we will only be able to cater for 5,000 at any one time. So it will have to be presented in stages. That's not SO bad, I guess?" Omha pulled a face at Cherry and grinned as his staff joined them. He needed time to digest this new request and walked swiftly towards the glass door. "I'm off, time to put my feet up for an hour or two." Omha removed his psychodelic apron from around his waist and hung it neatly behind the green door and made a quick exit before anyone could complain.

"How can you leave now?" Cherry chirped at him, running her hands through her hair as the spotted scarf flew across the room.

"There is always tomorrow." He rebuked over his shoulder then quickly disappeared. Omha sprinted up six flights of stairs to their spacious quarters which over-looked the Botanical gardens. He could have easily taken the air-lock but it was good exercise and released some of his frustration. After requesting a long refreshing drink from the fridge computer, Omha flung his lithe body into the comfort of a lazy-boy chair and pressed the buttons for massage and colour therapy. Then he waited patiently for his body to relax. The view was breath taking. He gazed out over the red planet and feasted his eyes on the horizon. Two pink moons glided into view. Omha's eyes lids soon grew heavy as he drifted into a meditative sleep.

Much later, Cherry closed the door quietly and she tiptoed across the marble floor and slipped into their sleeping quarters, "I will leave Omha in peace tonight and with any luck he would find a solution to this present situation." She whispered to herself and quickly drifted off into a deep sleep.

The following morning Omha arrived at the complex full of new ideas. "Cherry my dear, will you ask the staff to assemble before they start today's menu. Please! Sorry, I am so excited I nearly forgot my manners. Good morning my dear. Thank you for allowing me to sleep peacefully last night, it was much appreciated." He planted a warm kiss on her cheek.

"Okay everyone gather around. Omha wants to speak to you all. Now! I think he has had a brain-wave about the menu for the gathering." announced Cherry, surprised at Omha's refreshed energetic disposition.

"How are we all this fine morning? Are you all here?" Omha started counting heads. "One, two …Seventeen, eighteen. Where's Dot?"

"I'm coming, I coming." Dot dashed through the swing doors straightening her cap, smiling at everyone. "Did I hear Omha had a brainwave?" She teased with a giggle, as she smoothed her apron.

"Now as you have heard there will be a ***grand gathering*** later this month and we have to find a solution to feeding 144,000 souls. A bit mind bending; even for professionals like us." He puffed out his chest with pride. "But guess what? I had a profound dream last night and now have the perfect answer. Are you ready?" Omha's face was shinning with enthusiasm as he quizzed the group of listeners and they all nodded with expectation.

"Soel and Solina have created a theme for this rescue mission which was to be a Celestial Barbecue but when I researched how we could possibly accommodate such a tall order, it became impossible. So I have changed the menu just a tad. We are now going to serve Celestial Kebabs and Angel Cakes. Why?" Pause. "Because we can incorporate some very special ingredients in the recipes, last night I received a vision. Are you ready?"

"What do you mean by, special ingredients?" Catrina requested eager to know some of the mystery secrets.

"You will all find out in good time. First we must get on with the preparations and I must visit Soel to give him the good news and share my intentions." A few hours later Omha returned to the preparation centre with a big smile and requested that his staff assemble once again to hear about the forth coming preparations.

"Now here are the recipes we are going to use for the big day."

RECIPE

- 10 kg Chicken mince
- 1 kg Lotus flowers
- ½ cup Sesame seeds
- 3 tbps Paprika
- 1 kg Cornmeal
- 3 pkts Seaweed   100 Turkish Rolls
- 36 Shallots   10 bottles Tamarillo Sauce
- 2 tbps Garlic   10 Lettuce
- Cosmic ingredient

"Each one of you will mix these ingredients in a large glass bowl. Then roll out portions sizes into sausage shapes. These will be cooked on a barbecue in advance and stored in the cooler. On the day they will be placed in the Turkish rolls with Tamarillo sauce. We will garnish them with lettuce leaves and Venusian Forget-Me-Knots; these will be assembled on the day. I will order the ingredients today and we will be able to start preparing tomorrow, Any questions?" Omha peered around the room at the keen faces, patiently waiting to reply to any smart comments.

"Yes! That won't be enough to keep them happy." Dot pipped up.

"Each volunteer will be served two rolls each." Omha stated calmly. "Quite a meal if I say so myself and full of nourishment for the journey." Omha stood still and rubbed his hands together in satisfaction. "Ah! But there is more dear ones! I have a few more surprises in store. A grand finishing touch! . . . And IT is delicious. When all this is prepared I will inform you of the next stage. So off you go, there is plenty to do in the mean time." Omha smiled to himself, he was pleased with the vision he had received the night before.

ASTRODOME

High above the roof of the Astrodome, the heliport became quickly congested with craft and space shuttles. Parking was at a premium. Stressed traffic controllers had never witnessed so many visitors arriving at one time from across the Universe.

"Zak there's another Aero-bus due in ten seconds. Do we have a space allotted for them?" Tok scanned the parking screen.

"Yes, just give me a moment to direct the Master of Ceremonies into his reserved bay," replied Tok, intent on giving directions. "It's the brass!"

"Okay but hurry. This huge craft has gathered the flock from around the galaxy and we have to off load a thousand folks this time. I need the right docking bay for them to disembark."

Tok was involved with communications to another pilot, "Okay, I have a space for you now Sir. Please continue towards No 1 docking bay beside the Astra Building, it has been prepared for your arrival."

"Is there a space now?" enquired Zak urgently.

"Yes, yes! We made it. Direct the Aero-bus to No 13. The pathway is clear now." Tok breathed deeply relieved that all the flights had been accommodated. "How many more do you estimate?"

"That's about the last of them for now. You can take a break." Zak fell back in his chair quite exhausted with the sheer volume of crafts arriving at one time. But out the corner of his eye he caught a glimpse of yet another craft on his edge of the screen which carried the emblem of hierarchy.

"Sorry Tok there's another space shuttle arriving. Those refreshments will have to wait a bit longer. Quick, take a scan and find them a landing!" Zak quickly inspected the five screens.

"I don't know if there is one available. Who is it anyway?" Tok diligently searched the docking bays. The screen filled up with the masses of people walking towards the entrance of the building. "We will have to ask them to HOLD for now until it's clear."

"Okay."

"Who is it anyway? I thought all the brass had arrived." Tok moved closer to peer over Zak's shoulder trying to make out the emblem etched on the shuttle but the information had quickly switched over to the Security channel.

"It's Schumann, the Governor from the Galactic Federation, arriving from Sirius!" stated Zak turning to look at Tok searching his face for an answer. "We haven't made preparation. No one mentioned he was attending this conference."

"What will we do?" whispered Tok and then quickly returned to the communication link.

"Good morning Sir, we were not notified of your invitation to attend." Zak spoke respectfully. "Can you please hold while we make the appropriate arrangements?"

"No problem Control. Put you on your toes, eh!" There was humour in Schumann's voice. Two minutes passed and Tok became agitated as he diligently searched the screen for a docking bay.

"It's no good, all floors are full. What will we do now?" Zak pleaded for help from his co-worker but didn't wait for a reply. Zak made an executive decision, "Schumann, please proceed to the private quarters of the Master's docking bay at the left side of the Astrodome. There will be a contingence to meet you, Sir. I have made the appropriate arrangements. Will there be anything else?"

"Thank you, Control. My mission is top secret, that's why you were not informed of my intended visit. The dark forces are on watch at present and I didn't want to alert them to our presence in this sector or of the assembly." Schumann replied sternly. "So I would appreciate it if you kept this information under your hat for now."

"Yes Sir, understood. I will attend to your quarters myself. See you in 10 minutes." Zak let out a sign of relief. "Tok, I will have to leave you on watch, I think we have achieved a small miracle this day. Thank you for your patience during this fiasco, we did well. Now I must go and make preparations for our eminent guest."

RECEPTION HALL 4

Esha walked confidently into the large reception hall looking for refreshments, hoping to connect with old comrades. It had been a few light years since they had all parted for new destinations. After collecting a large glass of fresh fruit juice, Esha selected a table where she could observe the crowd filing into the room. And then she recognized a bubbling laugh coming from the mist of the crowd.

"Petra! Is that you?" Esha's voice carried across the room as Petra surveyed the countless faces, moving slowly amongst the crowd. Esha reached out and grabbed her by the hand. "I've been watching to see if you and the gang where invited."

"What do you mean invited?" Petra giggled, her smile had not changed and her effervescence was still deliciously contagious. "We were asked to volunteer. Can you believe that?"

"Are the others coming on this journey? Have you been in contact with them?" Esha was excited to hear the up-to-dated news.

"Can I please just go and get some refreshment and then we will exchange news?" Petra disappeared amongst the crowd again, heading directly for the juice bar.

Esha continued surveying the massing crowds, searching for Joel and Liam.

Petra flung her lithe body on the chair, "I'm back. I had no idea there would be so many folks gathering today. There must be a *real* panic on. We usually just meet on our own planet." Petra drank from the large, blue crystal container. "Um, that's nice."

"Is Jacob coming too? I've been looking out for the others, so far, no sign of them." Petra was listening but her attention was trying to identify the combination of flavours that invaded her senses. She peeped over her container watching Esha's face which still looked so youthful after many difficult and testing lifetimes mastering Earth duality. The Goddess energy had sustained her through the rough patches and love had blessed her with dedication to teaching the old practices.

"Why don't we tune-in like we used to when we wanted to make contact. Give them a signal where we are." Petra's mischievous violet eyes peered over the container. Although her present life had been full of many challenges she had missed having her team mates around.

At that moment a modulated voice sounded on the communication system and announced. "The first meeting to introduce you to this urgent assignment will be situated at

the Rose Bowl at 11 a.m. Please be seated by 10:45. You have all been allocated seating. Please use your pass number from the flight plan, when you arrived this morning."

"Okay we have one hour to try and find our friends amongst this massive crowd. Are you going to help me?" Esha commented, peering around the room and starting to feel uncomfortable by the sheer volume of people.

"What was that special signal we set up during our last stay on Earth? Wait, wait it's coming back to me now….." Petra could hear the wheels turning, searching to locate the memory.

"Wasn't it something like…Alfa and Omega!" Esha had suddenly remembered and her face lite up with a wide grin.

"Okay, hand on heart, mind in gear. Let's send out the signal together." Esha smiled and closed her eyes, mentally sending out the message along the spider's web that linked them from days gone and lifetimes together.

The two girls sat quietly amongst the hustle and bustle of the crowd determined to connect to their fellow travellers. They had shared many a lifetime, in different countries and locations on Earth, while perfecting the teachings and initiations of varied disciplines. Esha and Petra had assumed that their friends would feel duty bound to be part of this rescue mission, but now they were no so sure.

"What if they are not coming or they have to complete their present contracts elsewhere?" Esha sighed, her face looking disappointed.

"I bet they manage to wriggle out of them somehow, that wouldn't stop them being here. We have always gone on the important missions together as a support team. They will be here, I just know it!" Petra assured her by reaching out to touch her companion's hand. As they sat in their inner silence, connected to each other, someone behind them tripped over the leg of Esha's chair and bought the girls back to the present moment with a bang.

"Oh, must you be so clumsy! Didn't you see me sitting here!" chided Petra and turned to survey the culprit. "Jacob is that you?"

"Yes, I felt the call and was so busy trying to locate it's origin that I wasn't looking where I was going. And I was very curious to find out who it was. I thought our mob would be here and I was so sure that I would find you.

Where are all the others?" Jacob smiled with relief and fell into a bear hug with Esha then turned to Petra and nearly smothered her with his broad shoulders.

"Well, that's just what we were doing, trying to make contact. We were sure that you would all sign up for this mission. Have you seen anyone else?" Esha smiled sweetly, relieved to have found one of her companions.

"No not yet, I only arrived 10 minutes ago. But I felt sure I'd find some of you here and then I felt that heart connection. And here I am. Well, that still works for us after all these years, just shows you how strong our bond became over time. If it worked for me, then we will see the others arrive very soon. So let's sit tight and see who turns up next!" Jacob rambled excited at meeting up with his faithful friends once again. The three companions just sat and looked at each other. Over near the entrance there was a disturbance, as four new figures entered the room and made a bee-line straight for their table.

"Liam, Ruth, Tyler and Tamara! You are here! We have been sending out our old signal to let you know where we were. I just knew you would sign up! But where is Isobel?" The friends were full of questions and the greetings continued.

"Do you think Isobel will come? Does anyone know where her last assignment was? She became a brilliant teacher with disabled children maybe she became committed to the little ones. I really thought she'd be here," announced Joel with a disappointed tone in his voice.

"Well, maybe we will see her at the Rose Bowl," stated Tyler. "Cheer up."

"Okay you guys we only have a short time before we have to be seated. Have you all got your passes ready?" asked Ruth looking into their happy faces. Her mothering skills still remained very prominent in her character, at different time lines these friends had all been her children.

"How far is it from here?" Esha looked around hoping that someone knew the way.

"Not far. If we follow the others down that tunnel, we can't go wrong." Tyler had been observing the crowd as they generated to the large opening at the end of the long corridor.

"Come on, we don't want to be late."

The friends were joyful to just be together again as they linked arms.

"Did you see that brochure? Smashing eh! Someone did a great job putting that together. They used all the trappings under the Earth Sun. Can't say I visited any those exciting places on my recent missions. Families grew up, worked hard, married the girl down the road and raised their children in the town of their birth. I don't expect to travel that much this time either but one never knows. Maybe we will be stationed in a new location. I bet the mode of transport has improved." Liam chattered away thinking aloud.

The tunnel led them to a grand auditorium, larger than they had ever experienced before.

"Wow! How many did they invite? Must be thousands here......How are we going to find Isobel amongst this crowd?" The friends went in search of their allotted seats.

"Here we are! Look what a coincidence they have placed us all together." After they were all dully seated they realized there was one empty seat. "This means that Isobel will be here after all," cooed Ruth. "I'm so glad we will all be together, even if it's only for a short time. We must make the most of it. I know it's all about serious stuff, but let's have some fun too."

"I don't know if we will have time for fun. We only have 48 hours to be instructed about this mission and that doesn't seem very long, especially if it's critical. We might decide not to sign up." Liam informed them, trying to leave his options open.

"But if we all decide to take up this mission, you will come with us, won't you?" Petra pushed for an answer because it just wouldn't work out as planned if Liam decided to decline.

"Let's wait until we have more information. After this assembly things will be a lot clearer and we can make informative choices." Liam tried to smooth over the situation with a steady voice but Petra began to feel uncomfortable at the thought of leaving Liam behind.

"Look, there she is, coming our way!" The friends all waved frantically to guide Isobel to where they were sitting. Hugs were exchanged quickly, just in time before the gong sounded.

Jacob whispered in her ear, "It would not have been the same without you. I am so relieved that you decided to join us." And he reached over to clasp her hand tightly. "I was apprehensive that you had not received an invitation to this great gathering. That you may have already been committed to the new Genesis and I know how exciting and attractive that experiment would appeal to you."

"I'm here now Jacob, all will be well." Isobel planted a quick kiss on his cheek and turned her attention to the stage. The lights dimmed as the chairman of the Galactic Federation marched up to the rostrum.

ROSE BOWL

**The Chairman of the Galactic Federation
stood quietly before the Assembly.**

"Today we welcome each and everyone one for presenting yourselves here. As was mentioned on your invitation, we have asked for volunteers for a very serious situation that has been bought to our attention. Planet Earth has reached a critical stage of evolvement. We have all experienced the state of duality that operates in the third dimension, where it is crucial for positive and negative to maintain a balance for this planet to resume a healthy community and social well being.

As you know, we cannot interfere with the planet of ***free will.*** As the guardians of this Genesis we are bound to be of assistance when the inhabitants have gone beyond the fail- safe marker.

There are scientist and prestigious leaders who have taken it into their own hands to create dissention between land ownership and boundaries. There have been thousands slaughtered in the name of religion. We have witnessed this through the ages. Last month as we were preparing to review Planet Earth's progress, we were put on alert to a very disturbing faction and now there is another World War in progress. Many have lost faith, thousands have lost their lives and a great number will not survive the psychic trauma of the aftermath.

The Crimson Council conferred with the Galactic Federation and between us we have devised a new plan to assist Earth in the near future. If Earth's inhabitants continue on their present pathway, they will reach termination by the year 1999. Of course this is one potential that we desperately hope to avoid. As you will all remember in our history scrolls, Earth has already experienced termination twice before under catastrophic circumstances and it took hundreds of years for the Earth and her people to recover. This present scenario must be avoided at all costs. For it is time indeed, for these souls experiencing duality to mature and move through the next octave of soul evolution and consciously remember they are divine beings.

This is why we have sent out the call to those of you who have moved through to the fifth dimensional level of energy, wisdom and knowledge.

'The call is to assist and teach with love and compassion'. In the near future the populace will face graver situations than we have seen present today. So we the **Council** have been preparing a novel strategy to save them from the Dark Forces and put into place a new program from this day forward.

You the devoted ones, who remember the energy of Earth, still have families struggling to master the emotional, mental and spiritual lessons. This is why we have asked you to come forward and assist us with this new mission."

The crowd sat quietly waiting for him to resume, while he reached for a glass of water.

"Once again I ask you to carefully consider all I have spoken about. Your task will be extremely testing. Remember, once you pass through the birth process you will receive the veil of forgetfulness. Now I will hand you over to the Administrator."

An elderly Sage slowly shuffled to the Rostrum.

"Welcome! To you all, on this auspicious occasion of the great gathering! A gathering of so many, we have not witnessed before. If it were not for such a distressing situation you would make my heart sing." The Sage stood quietly, leaning on his staff for support, observing the sea of youthful faces that waited expectantly on his every word and the tears welled up in his eyes. He was already acutely aware of the tremendous task that lay before them and deeply admired their courage and determination. "Congratulations to each and every one of you, for having the courage to step forward during these troublesome times. A time in which we hope you will pledge your energy and take a momentous step forward, in the name of **Spirit**. Especially as you are all well versed in the trappings of the physical and emotional games of duality, we salute you.

We, the Council will assist you in all ways possible and each of you will have a team of unseen helpers that will guide your chosen journey. From this side of the veil we will love you and protect your footsteps, provide new data and teach you new procedures for the human condition. While you sit before me with your collective knowledge, I remind you that some of this information maybe difficult to recall in human form. So I now assure you that you will discover methods to access your soul knowledge. Many of you will become respected teachers and healers, this is your mission.

Your task will also include bringing enlightenment to the masses of the Truth. Do not expect to be welcomed with open arms by the establishment; your energy will make them feel threatened because you will demand change. You will be known as the **first wave**. These are preventative measures for the potentials we see in the near future." The Sage changed his stance and leaned heavily on the rostrum, taking a deep breath to centre his energy and then continued.

"In our original creation of a planet with **free will** we could not have foretold the outcome or the fact that it would draw inhabitants from many other sectors of the universe. Our vision was to create the most diverse planet with unique specimens of fauna and flora from near and far. This we achieved but the dynamics are sensitive to the whole balance. And as we speak, the balance is being threatened on many levels. We ask you to contemplate the severity of the problems set before you while formulating your choices.

During the next 24 hours we ask you to choose wisely. From here you will venture to the room of *'Free Choice'* to determine your journey and with whom you will travel. This procedure is already familiar to you, and you know how this operates. You have done this many times before.

We ask you to consider all avenues before committing yourselves to this cosmic mission. Discuss any queries you have with your friends during the rest period. Seek out your mentors for advice on any particular avenue that you feel uncertain about. Refreshments will be served in the Reception Hall at 6p.m. We shall gather together once more tomorrow at 11a.m. to view the courageous ones who choose to take up this most dedicated, mission. We thank you."

There was a hushed silence of respect as the Sage shuffled off the stage to take his seat among the elite Ones.

The crowd slowly dispersed to discover their respective sleeping quarters, to meditate on the uncertainty of their future choices. Some would not return on the morrow. Some would hesitate and seek council from their elders. Many would take up the Sword of Truth, the Armour of Wisdom and the Staff of Justice, to wear the Cloak of Love and Compassion.

ORIENTATION 6 ROOM

A modulated voice informed the volunteers of preparation schedules.

"Our facilities can only accommodate 5,000 at one sitting. We have divided each sitting into 'pods'. These 'pods' will concur with your invitation cards that present in your sleeping quarters. The first orientation block will be those whose invitation ends with the No 1. Each 'pod' will follow in numerical order throughout the afternoon at 2 hourly intervals, please be prepared for your orientation and wait patiently in line. Block 1 will commence at 3p.m. Block 2 will commence at 5p.m and so on. Thank you for your attention."

Our group of friends observed the timetable and inspected their invitation cards to check which Block they needed to attend.

"Well look at that, we all have the same number. That is SO good," Ruth exclaimed. "For a moment I thought we were going to be separated."

"Yeah! That means we will all return into the same time frame. Have you decided which part of the world you are going to birth in?" Liam queried, eagerly watching his friends faces for a response.

"I haven't got that far yet. So let's start at the beginning, have you all decided to take up the challenge?" asked Petra gazing into their eyes, waiting for a chorus of the enthusiastic reply of 'yes! Yes!'

"It will be so exciting if we are all going at the same time," Ruth's eyes were shining with anticipation of what could be, as she jumped up and down on the spot.

Tyler stood silently listening to his companions, uneasy because he had been about to sign up for another experiment with his present delegation on Orion. "Well, we were about to go on a contemporary assignment to the New Earth. I was really wrapt with engineering some of the advanced ecology that was being planned." He looked at their disappointed faces. "But, if all you guys are going to front up I guess...........I might join you."

"Great! It wouldn't be the same if you weren't there. I love your energy and God knows we are going to need all the help we can get." Stated Jacob, he reached over and gave his friend a warm hug.

"Esha, you have been very quiet, what do you feel is right for you?" Isobel gazed into her eyes and saw a small shadow of doubt.

This gentle soul had been mentally reviewing the Sage's introduction and wondered if this journey would really be her next best step. Her last incarnation had been a lonely road but she had mastered the conditions of her trials and tribulations. Found her God-self.

"I have only recently returned to this peaceful dimensional plane. Just a few months ago. It's nice to feel the comfort of family around me. Do I really want to leave them and go on another, adventure? Maybe I'm pushing myself to hard if I decide to return so soon?" she gazed at the solemn faces, looking for support.

"Hey, we will all be there to help you. How could we leave you here? It just wouldn't be the same. Besides, I have a great idea, what if you and I became partners this time. What do you say? Come on Esha. If you agree, I *promise* to be there for you, every step of the way." pleaded Jacob. He stood patiently beside her, touching her elbow with focus and intention, hardly daring to hear her reply. All their friends waited with anticipation while Esha contemplated this latest piece of news.

"Well, what do you think?" Petra couldn't contain herself any longer.

"Come on, please be part of this journey with us," squealed Isobel, jumping up and down on the stop. "You have loved Jacob forever. This time you will be able to share so much more, a whole lifetime of loving!"

"Well that's settled then! We are all going to return. If we keep focused, and remember that we *will* find each other, there's no problem," stated Liam with his optimist nature.

"Okay, I promise to discuss the whole situation with Jacob."

"Okay, let's go find our sleeping quarters and we'll meet back here at 3 p.m." Tyler instructed calling over his shoulder, as he headed down the long corridor. He too, needed time alone to think clearly and make a positive decision. If he decided to take this mission, he would have to apply for a leave of absence from Orion.

"I think I need some fresh air. Ruth, do you want to come and sit in the garden with me? I have an urgent need for some space and to meditate amongst that beautiful botanical fragrance, it always helps me think more clearly. Are you coming?" requested Petra.

"Why not, we can listen to the celestial notes and bring in a little more balance while making a rational decision. It's just too noisy here to think straight."

The group dispersed to go their separate ways. "See you at 3 p.m." Came the chorus of jubilant voices as they scattered in different directions.

Block 1 – 3 p.m.

"Although we have asked you to return to one of the most beautiful planets, we give you warning that there will be many challenges waiting for you during this future lifetime. We the Council and Federation give heart felt 'thanks' that your courageous hearts are prepared to venture forth on this journey. You will encounter many new challenges. I will now introduce you to the Master that will conduct this Forum. Please welcome Master Abra."

A tall distinguished man with red hair dressed in a dark crimson robe walked quickly to the centre of the stage and bowed to his audience, to honour their presence.

"As you know we have this small – *but very special* – planet that is dear to our hearts, the planet called Earth that spins at the outer edge of this galaxy. This is the greatest learning school of opposites where we go to master emotion and duality. It is quite unique and extremely breathtaking. Teeming with hundreds and thousands of different life forms, it incorporates the very highest and lowest frequencies known in the cosmos."

Master Abra's face was shinning with wonderment, he had just finished reviewing the brochure that Soel and Soleina had formatted as an invitation to this collective audience.

"Our people on Earth are incredibly beautiful life forms and are capable of carrying the highest frequencies of love, light and joy known throughout the Universe. On the other hand they are also capable of carrying the dense and darkest frequencies the cosmos has ever experienced – frequencies that the rest of creation at some point in time will have the opportunity of mastering, in preparation for evolvement."

Master Abra looked out upon the assembled volunteers and the many shining faces, and smiled quietly to himself. "Hum!" and took a breath.

"Here is the current situation. Within the domain of time, as this planet passes through cosmic cycles, it is reaching a point of maturity. It is now approaching the end of two major cycles – the 2,000 year Age of Pisces and a 26,000 astrological year as it journeys around the central Sun of the Milky Way galaxy.

With the completion of any cycle, many phases are coming to an end and preparation is being made for new beginnings. More importantly, the planet is experiencing an infusion of light as it aligns to pass through the Photon Belt. This will dramatically change and INCREASE THE FREQUENCY AND VIBRATION of Earth. During major times of transition, there will always be a certain amount of turbulence. Earth herself is a living being and is also evolving, so there will be great geological and climate changes.

This will not be a particularly easy time for humans, especially those who are still unaware of their spiritual nature. But more specifically, for those who are operating and vibrating at the lower frequencies. With the frequency changes, many will be confronted with their insecurities, which may in turn create frustration, anger and fear. The Human heart is not comfortable with Change."

Master Abra walked deliberately across the stage, hands locked behind his back, looking at the marble floor. Then turned and retraced His steps.

"The first era of evolution on this planet was the physical, a time of survival. The second era which is now coming to an end is the mental era that incorporated logic and industrialisation. The third era that will begin at the passing of the marker, the year 2,000, will be the time of the *heart* to generate peaceful co-existence and the flowering of love for one another. This is the highest frequency and it will require some considerable length of time to perfect the changes. It will not happen over night.

Those who currently hold the reign of power on the Planet are of the *old order* of the physical and mental. Many who have already committed to hold the Light are capable of making a graceful transition to the heart-centre and a divinely guided life, they will find this a smooth transition. Those who are stuck in the old energy will experience much turmoil. This is the present situation.

We are here today to seek volunteers who would be willing to incarnate at this present time to assist in creating a smooth transition for the masses. In the past we have sent prophets and teachers, very often they were persecuted and killed for speaking of the Universal Truths.

Many, of these so called enlightened beings were coerced into building religions and rituals around the teachings of the day because their egos overruled their intentions and these religions were used to control others. So this time we are trying a different approach.

No more prophets, saviours and avatars that the dark forces can use to create more religions. This time we are sending forth thousands of extraordinary Light Beings, who will guide and teach the truth. You will only have two assignments. '*To stay in your heart energy, regardless of your life experiences, and to remain in your truth and integrity*'.

NOW THAT SOUNDS EASY ENOUGH, RIGHT?

Unfortunately, this will not be an trouble-free assignment. Why? Duality has reached its peak of excellence on planet Earth. Man has perfected the illusion of good and evil. The greatest difficulty will be to remember Who You Really Are, Why You Are There and What This Mission Is Really About. At your time of remembering you will be able to stay in your heart centre, regardless of external events.

So how will you know when you are remembering? The moment you become aware that you are in a place of judgment, you will know you have been sleeping, and you will remember Who You Really Are. That will be your signal." Master Abra stood still and took a deep breath.

"Now here is the challenge: Throughout your life you will need to learn about discernment – to evaluate what is true, what is appropriate and what is paramount for the Greatest Good of All, both for yourself and the Planet. Discernment is similar to judgment; here there is a fine line. However, you will know when you are in judgment and when you have moved out of your heart centre, and that will be when you are in a place of blame.

We know how challenging this mission will be. We understand how very real the illusions will appear to be, the incredible density of this dimension and the pressures you will be faced with. If you survive this mission, and we remind you that it is a voluntary one – you will evolve rapidly through continuous dimensional shifts.

We also give another caution here; that some of you, who return to Earth as star seeds, may never have the opportunity to germinate. We will welcome you home as a hero for trying. Some of you will awaken and begin to shine, only to be choked and destroyed by opinions and the prevailing thought forms around you. Others will awaken and remain awake and your Light will become a source of inspiration and remembrance of the ones who sit on these chairs, because many who have been friends and family will be watching you from the Gallery and cheering you on.

You will incarnate all over the planet – in every culture, every race, every country and infiltrate every religion. *You will be different. You will never quite fit in.*

As you awaken, you will realize that your true family isn't necessarily those of your own belief, culture, country and race. Even those from your biological family will sometimes feel foreign. You may even doubt that you are in the right place at the right time and ask *'am I on the right planet?'* And you will look for your Cosmic family (the ones who sit beside now in this room) – those who have come as you came, on assignment to assist in ways large and small in the current transition. True brotherhood in its highest form will come only in remembering Who You Really Are, Why You Are Here and What This Lifetime is Really About.

It will become a real awakening as you return to the true Temple of Divinity, ***your heart.*** When this remembrance takes place, you will understand that you volunteered to **serve** the Earth world."

So, are you ready brave Souls?

A bright smile crossed Master Abra's face and reached his eyes, they gleamed with light, a light that reached every soul in the audience.

"So there are a couple of other minor things I should mention, just in case you have forgotten the procedure and I sincerely hope it doesn't sway your present decision to be of service to Spirit. A quick reminder folks!

On arrival to the Earth planet, you will slide down a small tunnel into a bright light, were you will be clothed with a biological suit which will pass through many physical changes during your lifetime. This biological suit is simply a vehicle while in the third dimension. You are not your biology, you are unique. However because this is a planet of duality – there is a DANGER that you will forget who you really are! There are two basic categories called **genders**. In order to operate within the third dimension, you will receive a microchip called **personality**. This is like an identity imprint and along with your biological suit will allow you to participate in the hologram there called **consensus reality.**

You may even come to believe you are your personality. This might sound outrageous right now, so once again we remind you to tap into your **heart self.**

There is SO much we could instruct you in but we have great faith in you and believe in your good intentions, because you have already passed through this procedure many times before. We congratulate each and everyone who is prepared to venture forward. You are our HOPE and we salute you. As you grow into maturity and take up new views, see beyond the rigid boundaries, and embrace forward thinking opportunities that will carry mankind forward – you will be known as the 'Enlightened Ones' and the 'Awakened Souls' or such similar terms.

We the Galactic Federation and Crimson Council, thank you. Blessings until we meet again."

Master Abra placed his hands on his heart and took a deep breath then throwing open his arms he cast forward a Ray of White Light which drifted like a mist amongst those gathered and towards each person present to be absorbed into their soul centre.

7
FREE CHOICE ROOM

The friends filed out of the Orientation Room and collectively headed to the Reception Hall for refreshments. Each member of the team moved slowly, deep in thought, not daring to look at one another.

"Let's find our table, the one where we met up this morning," suggested Tyler breaking the silence.

They all seated themselves and then looked expectantly at one another waiting for the first one to speak.

"Well, that gives us some extra information to add to the 'Brochure'. Does it sound as exciting as it did this morning?" Petra asked, peering into the silent youthful faces, waiting for a reply.

"Come on, someone say something. Do you still think you can handle this mission?" Liam requested in a sombre voice.

"I'm going for some refreshments, everyone want some?" inquired Joel. "Raise your hands. Everyone want the same? Okay that's eight, I'll be back soon." Suddenly, they were all talking at once.

"Are you really sure about this?"

"What do you really feel? Is it a good idea?"

"I'd forgotten how tough it was to be in third dimension."

"Yes, but we did agree to go together."

"Why, are you thinking of backing out now?"

"Hey! One at a time, I can hardly hear myself think. Let's wait for Joel to return."

The friends fell silent again, receding back into their private thoughts. Ten minutes later Joel found his way back to the table laden with a tray of large glasses.

"So what's happening? Did you discuss anything in my absence?" His face was beaming with enthusiasm, impatient to discover their opinions and suggestions for the future.

"No, we decided to wait for your return," replied Ruth solemnly.

"Well, I still feel positive about this adventure, especially if we are all going to be together again. That will make it unusually exciting, don't you think?" he smiled at each one. "Don't all talk at once? Cat cut your tongue?" Joel sat down and waited patiently, his chin in his hands observing their troubled faces.

"I'll go first, then. We were just saying how much we had forgotten what it was like. You know all that personality stuff!" remarked Liam with a disheartened tone. "When we are here we can just be ourselves."

"Yes, but that depends on what we choose before we leave this place. What we have to think about is which astrological sign would fit us best for this particular mission. You know the energies of each sign. Leo, Aries and Sagittarius or Pisces, Virgo and Capricorn etc And then, we have to research which sign will match up with the person we are going to meet up with when we get to our destinations," explained Ruth trying to be logical.

"Getting very complicated for me," Esha sighed looking confused.

"Well, not really. I did heaps of extensive study in astronomy and astrology last lifetime, so I can assist you guys with making those decisions. That should be a lot of fun. We could do that tonight, if you want some sound insights." Jacob offered, smiling at the forlorn faces. "Come on, cheer up, its not so difficult. I'll research some of my data. In the meantime how about we find some of that enthusiasm you had this morning. After all that's why we met up again. What do you reckon, let's all go one more time?"

"What time do we have to be in Room 7 to submit our *future life* because I need some serious meditation to get my head straight before I make a commitment," Tamara instinctively knew she needed a quiet place to think.

"I'm pretty sure we don't have to sign up until the morning and we can do that on our personal crystal screen in our sleeping quarters, but only when we are positive about we are all going." Ruth decided to buy some time to think things through.

"So I will see you later in the 'chat-room' on level 16 at 9p.m. Okay?" Joel pushed for an agreement from his friends, with a big smile on his face, while nodding his head.

"Okay, yes we will be there," came the chorus. "See you then but you better have some great information on how to get this right."

The friends dispersed to their respective sleeping quarters to meditate on future conditions for their impending return to Earth. Each one acknowledged how difficult their last journey had been and now here they were contemplating another return. How quickly things can change, just when you think you have made a decision! But when they heard the *'call'* their compassion over rode all their good intentions. They had all felt the urgency of the communication, like a strong heartbeat. Once again the beautiful planet drew them back like a magnet. The splendour of the mountains, rivers, valleys, sunsets and fauna, no other planet offered such an array of precious colours and fragrances. Now they had to contemplate the physical reality of returning to play out the dramas that may or may not turn a world in turmoil into a potential place of peace and goodwill. It was a big *ask*. Each one knew they could not achieve this on their own merit. But as a collective, with 144,000 other Light Beings then all things were possible.

Chat Room, 9p.m.

Ruth stuck her head gingerly around the corner and found the room empty.

"I guess I'm the first one. I hope the others are going to show up." She muttered to herself, sitting in the chair closest to the door so she could make a quick escape. Ruth studied the brochure of the Blue Planet and reminisced over its beauty.

Ten minutes later another face peered into the room, relieved to see a friendly face. "I wasn't sure if anyone was going to be here after that last conversation we had," said Liam with a sigh. "I'm so glad I found you here. Have you received any bright ideas?"

Ruth was about to reply when the others burst into the room full of apologies for being late, "Sorry, we got caught up and didn't realise the time." Each one scrambled for a chair. With their energies replenished, smiles on their faces and a happy mood of expectation, they were prepared for some serious discussion.

"Jacob, how did you go with that astrology information? We need to study it carefully." Petra enquired, as she glided towards the neat pile of research papers on the glass-table top.

"Everything's in order. I spent time matching up the data and I think I have come up with some pretty good plans. Find the file with your name on it and spend a few minutes reviewing my suggestions. I think I know you all fairly well but feel free to make any changes you think will assist you. Did anyone have any suggestions about the time scale they preferred because I will have to alter the time / place of birth, if you have."

There was silence in the room as each one carefully studied their perspective future life with a fine toothcomb.

"May I interrupt for a moment? The next decision will be do you want to stay the same gender as you own, now?" Jacob threw down the gauntlet, and throwing back his head, he laughed out loud. "You should see your faces. Just when you thought you had all the information. Now you will have to choose who is who."

"That's not funny, Jacob. Look at all these pages we have to read and assimilate, we don't have a lot of time." Tamara chided him impatiently while waving the file at him.

"That's true but deciding what gender is quite important, don't you think?" Jacob tried to be serious for a brief moment. "There are certain implications about your relationships."

"I know!" Tamara continued with her study and then realised that her soul-mate was somewhere out there amongst the stars on his own mission. God knows where that was at this present time. She kept her thoughts to herself because for the life of her, she could not think of anyone else she would take this mission with. So where is Alistar?

8

PREPARATION ROOM

Meanwhile in the kitchen, all hands were called to be present for the celebration that was ordained for the coming day. For the last two days there had been a constant effort and concentration on the *special* ingredients for the 'Angel Cakes'. Although the Master Chef had started his recipe with a standard set of ingredients he had also included some extra components which he felt necessary to enhance the recipe.

"Matilda have you collected the stamen's from the water-lily's?"

"Yes chef, I have three baskets ready in the cooler," she replied with a big smile. "Do you want me to go and collect them, now?"

"In about half-an-hour, please Matilda."

"What are they for, sir?"

"To add perception to these courageous souls who have volunteered for a very unusual mission. But I have also included some other ingredients that we have not used before." Omha felt enormously pleased with his intuition.

"Martha do you have the chilli seeds ready? They will be for stamina."

"Yes chef. They didn't half make my eyes water. It took me a whole shift to do that!"

"Thank you Martha, I knew you would persevere." Omha smiled and gave her a nod of satisfaction.

"George, do you have the Geranium leaves, chopped finely?"

"Yes, there are two large bowls waiting. What are they for?" asked George begging to know the answer and quench his curiosity.

"I have included them for protection against negativity. These folks will have quite a battle with the negative forces within those long standing religious establishments and breaking through the dogmas."

"I can understand that very well, chef." George validated his boss.

"Now there is one ingredient missing but it must be gathered in the moonlight, tonight." Omha watched their reaction and waited.

"What is that?" they called out in unison.

"Will you ask John to be here at midnight and we will all go out together to collect Moon-drops. This unique essence will provide a perfect connection to home and create a fine web of communication with those guardians who will be watching over our brave travellers."

Omha felt satisfied. He had remembered everything that was necessary to sustain the pioneers on their hazardous mission.

"Oh, I nearly forgot the fifth element. Will you please ask Arthur if he has ground the Rose Quartz crystals into a fine powder? I'm sure he prepared it some weeks ago but I don't know where he stored it for safe keeping." Just at that moment Arthur walked into the kitchen with four clay pots neatly covered with a fine lawn fabric.

"Here they are Omha. I thought you would be requiring these very soon. Quite a job you set me. It took me until now to complete my task." Arthur was proud of the part he had been asked to attend to. Working with Rose Quartz was a privilege, such a gentle crystal, warm and nurturing to the heart. "This will strengthen the weakest link when it comes to loss. It will be very necessary for these folks this time around." Arthur had worked with crystals for as long as he could remember and was curious as to how the powder would be administered.

"What are you going to do with the Rose Quartz, Omha?" Arthur waited patiently. During the past two weeks while he worked with the Rose Quartz he had been intrigued as to how it would be included into a recipe.

"Well, it's a secret that was handed down to me by my teacher many light years ago and he showed me how it could be dissolved in a good red wine to enhance the energy of the elixir, to give it added properties. It only takes a few grains in each cup, so we will have plenty for tomorrow night's celebration." Omha explained earnestly, he had never shared the secret before with anyone but he felt obliged to honour Arthur with the trusted knowledge. Then he went to congratulate his staff members.

"You have all done a great job, thank you very much, I really appreciate all the effort you have put in over the past three weeks. Now you can all have your supper and then we will go and collect the Moon-drops at midnight."

"Well, we think you have done a magnificent job too. There was only a short time to prepare this menu. Well, done. We can all take a bow." His staff returned the praise. "Will you share supper with us?"

"Yes I would really like that. It's been a very trying few weeks."

Two hours later, the team returned to the kitchen and started to assemble the special recipe in extra large bowls. The ovens were made ready and they waited impatiently for the finished product to be lifted onto the benches to cool.

"Wow! They look magnificent, Omha!"

The team just stood and looked in amazement at the glowing cakes, they seemed to have an energy all of their own. The little cakes gleamed, a golden yellow, with frilly pink edges. The team had never seen such beautiful delicacies before.

"You've got a winner there, everyone will partake, I bet." hummed Arthur nodding his head, his eyes all a sparkle. "Can we try one now?" he teased Omha.

"Okay, just one each. But they are not quite complete yet. Tomorrow morning we will get the Jellybean machine working, my final touch. This will add an extra touch of humour to their essence. Jellybeans are such fun and come in a great choice of colours. God knows these folks will need a large dose of joy. Now, eat your cake. Then we will go and collect the moon drops. The Moons are full tonight and it's nearly time. I want the drops to be placed in the crystal vials on the bench."

The air was balmy as the group wandered through the Cherry orchard and they sang a harvest hymn as they moved amongst the trees.

"Don't the blossoms look divine in this light? It's like walking through Fairyland, makes me feel very special." Martha whispered to her friend.

"I know what you mean. I keep expecting to see the Fairy Queen and her entourage pop out from the nearest branch any moment. Wouldn't that be a treat?" Dot skilfully scooped up another Moon-drop into her crystal vial while peeping through the branches to gleam a tiny glimpse of the illusive fairy folk.

"Okay everyone back to the preparation room. I can see that your vials are almost full, I'm sure we will have sufficient for tomorrows needs."

The night was so beautiful that no one hurried. The cherry blossoms oozed a sweet aroma that hung in the ether like a delicate mist, renewing their senses into a state of euphoria.

"Time to rest before the busy day! Off you go now." Omha commanded.

"But!. . . What about the wine? Are we going to prepare it now?" Martha raised an eyebrow in expectation.

"No, that will be done just before it is served. That way the Moon-drops will hold their pure essence and be rich and silky smooth to drink. That can wait until tomorrow afternoon just before the orientation. Okay, farewell my fine friends, I will see you here at 5a.m. Rest well."

HEARTBEAT

Alistar had just departed from Pegasus to take a vacation on the New Earth Project. There had been wonderful reports of the updated matrix. The spacecraft had been programmed with the coordinates, so his mind relaxed into a meditative state of bliss. As he passed through the Milky Way he observed the magnificent colours of Nebulas and new stars being formed, cosmic dust coagulating to form and birth new galaxies. A euphoric peace entered his being. Space travel always presented his mind with possibilities for adventure beyond his knowing, there was no end to understanding how it had all formed in the beginning.

Suddenly he felt a ripple in the force, which brought his attention back to the control centre; there were no flashing lights or warning signals. The flight path was clear, no obstacles appeared within close range and the radar screen was not picking up any unidentified objects near his space module. Suddenly he clutched his heart charka; he had not felt that pain for many years, which could only mean one thing. Mentally he searched the airways for the unseen communication to make a connection.

"Tamara, are you okay?" Alistar sent a silent telepathic message across the airways. His soul-mate was in some kind of trouble.

"Where are you?" He waited with anticipation. It had been many moons since their last communication. Their love continued through the ages while each one attended to their specific missions.

Tamara sat quietly by the beachfront watching the two pink moons slide across the horizon as they kissed the crystal waters. She had been contemplating this mission to planet Earth and knew the importance of a good outcome. Conditions had become extremely unstable since her last journey there when Alistar and she took their final initiation in the Temple of Diana.

Tamara's heart felt an extra heartbeat and realized Alistar had tuned into her deepest concerns and she wondered where he was stationed at this moment.

"Alistar did you receive the Galactic Federation invitation for volunteers?

They are assembling the Peacemakers. Planet Earth sent out a red alert."

"Where are you, my precious? I felt your connection a few minutes ago and I've been waiting to understand your concerns." Alistair pleaded, hands now firmly on the controls.

"I am sitting on the beach at Alderbarren, trying to access whether to take this journey by myself. My heart tells me this is the next step for me. The gang is all here, they are going to sign up tomorrow, but I'm not sure about Esha. She too is still feeling a little uncertain but Jacob has suggested they go as partners. Together they will make a great team and maybe they will have the opportunity to take their final initiation." Alistar interrupted her chatter.

"Wow, take a breath." There was a pause. "No, I didn't hear about the call for volunteers, I was on station at Sirius. Now I'm on my way to the New Earth project."

Tamara's voice became soft and gentle, "Alistar, will you come on this mission with me? Can you break your contract? Please!"

"Give me ten minutes to think about it. I will have to connect to the Syrian Council to make arrangements for a replacement if I decided to change my plans," Alistair declared.

"So, you *really* will think about it? I'll wait here where there is a clear channel and enjoy the peaceful atmosphere. Thank you, Alistar!"

Tamara reflected on their past journeys together and the unconditional love that they had shared between lifetimes - the magic moment that led to their discovery of one another in the Temple of Isis. It had not always been a bed of roses. Many times they had incarnated separately and each lifetime had continued to be extremely lonely. Their hearts did not feel fulfilled, as they searched endlessly for each other. Alistair's voice bought her back to the present.

"Tamara! What is the deadline to register? I have permission to join the Peacemakers but it will take another five hours before I reach your destination," Alistar reported calmly.

"That's okay. We don't have to be present at the gathering until tomorrow at 11a.m. Thank you so much, my darling. You have made all the difference. I will meet you at the docking bay and then we can go to my sleeping unit and transcribe your entry form. So please think about – your new parents, education, race, creed and where we will join together in our future life. Things are going to get pretty tough on the Earth planet, so we need to cover all probabilities." she quickly informed him.

"That's a lot to think about, but I do remember the routine. I have enough time during the flight to make some notes and we can cross-reference them when I arrive. See you very soon, dear one, Transmission ending."

Tamara decided to stay on the beach, breathing in the sweetness. A pod of dolphins swam into the shallows and entertained her with their playfulness, proudly displaying their offspring and she enjoyed their communion for half an hour. Tamara saluted the pod calling each one by name. "Thank you for your company, I have to go now dear friends. I may not see you for some time, so wish me luck on this mission to planet Earth."

Tamara waved as she left the beach and returned to share the news with the gang. Her heart felt lighter now and she couldn't wait to see Alistar again. It was a good feeling, to know they would be sharing another life together.

Meanwhile Alistar contemplated the information he had just received from   Tamara and settled in front of the crystal screen and started to make a plan. He surprised himself by his quick response to her request because he thought he had the next few years mapped out but as they say on Earth, *'your luck can change in an instant.'*

Tamara wandered back along the pebble pathway through the lush greenery and tall trees. Peacocks and violet doves escorted her as far as the jasmine archway where they said their farewells. She knelt down and whispered, "I hope to see you all again when I return, until then I know you will watch over my friends in the Bay. We are all one family." Tamara skipped up the path and went straight to the chat-room, to join her friends, only to discover an empty room.

"I must find them and inform Jacob that Alistar will be part of the group. I wonder where they have all disappeared to." She clicked open the file on the crystal screen to see if anyone had left a message. "Retired to our sleeping quarters. See you at the Rose Bowl. P.S. Don't forget to submit your registration on Channel 6."

"I will have to wait for Alistar to arrive before I can totally complete all my details. I have four hours to wait. I'll go and rest." Tamara walked to her quarters and requested the computer to give her a wake-up call.

Each one in the group had returned to their private space after researching the past life information they had previously collected from the chat-room.

Now they had to prepare and submit their application form, having mapped out an outline that would blend experience and knowledge for their future life on planet Earth. There was much to consider.

ENTRANCE FORM

- Parents :   Mother :   Father :
- Personal Name :
- Gender :
- Siblings :
- Number of children in family :
- Life expectancy :

- Country of Origin :
- Language :
- Religious background :
  Astrological sign: Numerology:
  Financial status:
- Educational prospects :

- Marriage partner :
- Careers :

- Number of Children :
- Future destinations :

- Gifts :
- Guardians :
- Spiritual Teachers: Use by date :

MAIN PLAYERS

Esha / Jacob-   Background: Buddhist, of Asian decent.

Esha-   Chinese decent, born Hong Kong
Busy world, many people, and small family
Good education. Parent's own restaurant in Tokyo
Migrate to Australia 1978 to work in Perth

Jacob-   Vietnam, born in Saigon
Lives in small hut by the river, large family
Sneaks into public school to learn English.
Comes to Australia 1975 for education (scholarship)
Later moves to Margaret River, WA.

Petra / Liam-   Background: Roman Catholic, of Italian decent.

Petra-   Rome, born to rich parents, society people.
Large house, three children
Parents work in fashion industry.
Good education, later works as a designer.
Goes to Australia 1979 to live in Melbourne.

Liam-   Born in Tuscany, parents died during war - orphan.
Vineyard worker, prefers to be close to the earth.
Migrates to Australia 1972 to work in the Pilbara.

Ruth / Joel-   Background: Jewish faith. United Kingdom.

Ruth-   Father is a Banker in London, survived World War 11
Wife died in bombing, has only one daughter.

Lives with his Mother, to raise his child.
Educated in private school becomes a teacher
Migrates to Australia in 1965, in Sydney.

Joel- Lives in Wales and is expected to become a miner.
Parents escaped from Germany before uprising.
Mother not well, two brothers.
Lived in small town, with council education.
Arrives in Australia 1973 to work in Kalgoorlie.

Tamara and Alistar, Tyler and Isobel will be native residents and grow up in an Australian environment. They will experience a safe world, good job prospects, sandy beaches, blue skies and government education.

All are destined to meet in Australia. Connect to partners, settle and raise families. In their mid-forties they will move inter-state and finally meet up in Perth, which will be later known as *'The City of Light'* in the future.

EARLY MORNING 10

Tamara had spent the last two hours completing her application form trying to make some informative choices. There came a discreet quiet knock at her door. "Room service!"

"Who is it?" she whispered expecting to hear a male voice reply.

"I have a special treat for you." A small voice informed her from behind the closed door.

Tamara pressed the small blue button in the recess of the wall and the door quietly slide open to reveal Martha standing there with a big smile, offering a delicate cake on top of which sat a shiny jellybean, accompanied with a large glass of fruit juice.

"Thank you, this looks very inviting. Will everyone have one of these Martha?"

"Yes, the little cake is filled with a special blessing, for all those who are bound on this mission. We have been ever so busy in the kitchen making preparations." Martha, informed Tamara with a twinkle in her eye.

"Could you please leave an extra one here, I am expecting another member to arrive any time now. Alistar only heard about this mission late last night and is on his way to join us as we speak."

"Okay, I can fix that in no time at all," Martha disappeared down the corridor, soon returning with another small plate. "Here you go. Hope all goes well for you both."

Alistair requested a docking bay from the Control Room, and soon alighted from his craft. He headed straight for the Rest Room, he felt in great need of a shower and clean clothes. Alistair stepped up to the reception desk and politely requested the number of Tamara's quarters.

"Eleventh Floor, sir. Room 33. We have been expecting you, sir?" informed the desk clerk cheerfully holding out a glass plate key.

"Thank you. I received an urgent communication quite unexpectedly from my dear colleague about this gathering and now I am here." Alistar announced, for some unknown reason he felt he needed to explain himself.

"Bless you! Please take the lift to the left of the vestibule." The clerk pointed down the crimson-carpeted hallway, directing Alistair towards the right corridor.

Tamara had freshened up and tweaked her golden locks with crimson bows and was about to make her way to the docking bay when there was another soft knock on the door.

"Who is it?" When there was no answer, she quickly went to investigate and as the door opened, Alistar stood there with a big grin on his face.

"I made real good time and here I am!" Tamara flung her arms around his neck in sheer delight, their bond still alive after so many years apart.

"Come on, in. This is so good!" Her eyes were shining and her heart nearly jumping out of her chest. She stood back and just looked at him for a long moment. "I am so happy you decided to come on this mission. At the orientation, I realized this journey was a big ask, especially if I went alone. . . . I mean without you. Especially when we were told of the state of violence and unrest that Earth Planet had reached again. It reminded me of our last journey during the '*Spanish Inquisition,*' when more than a million women were slaughtered by the *church* for their so called 'magic powers and healing practices with herbs.'"

"Tamara, slow down. Are you telling me that it has really become that horrendous again?" Alistar's face looked shocked and sad as he slumped into a comfortable chair. Suddenly the joy of sharing a future lifetime with Tamara took on a different picture of what might be. After a moment he rallied and said, "Come on then share some of your predicted scenarios," he invited her as he tried to raise his tired body and then leaned back again as Tamara continued to verbalise her thoughts.

"Do you remember what happened to our friends when they returned from that time frame? We ALL had to go to the great pyramid on Sirius to enter the Healing Capsules and it took three months before we found our balance again. Then, another three months of counselling to align our mental bodies with our spiritual bodies. The trauma was SO great." Tamara stopped for a minute and took a breath, her face saddened by the memory. "That's why I called you. I didn't think it wise to go on this mission alone without you." A small crack of vulnerability sounded in her voice.

"Tamara I am getting the picture but you still haven't explained what the crisis is at the moment and what is perceived for the near future." Alistar tried to bring her attention back to the present task at hand.

"Sorry! I'm chattering away. Okay let me focus........There's World War II in progress. Scientists on two continents are getting close to discovering the universal numbers to create the 'atom bomb' and thousands of children are already living in poverty, despite the fact that there is enough food for every inhabitant on Earth." She stood still and drew in a deep breath.

"Once again the War Lords are hording funds for their private agendas. But wait there is more especially in the future as we move forward towards the turn of the century. Technology will advance at an extreme rate where governments, business co-operations and banking sectors will create a new world of fraud, espionage, and cyber cowboys. Many secrets will be revealed and the communication highways will uncover important deceptions within the above areas. More people will suffer from starvation and ethnic cleansing, by using biological warfare. Can you believe that! While tribal factions increase the unrest between neighbouring countries, multinationals encourage and conspire to deliver huge supplies of *nuclear* arsenal."

"Wow! Take another breath." Alistar reached over and touched her arm he could see that she was very agitated and close to tears, becoming far too emotionally involved.

"We both understand how much more we can achieve when our energies are working together on the planet. We bring in a balance, where we can see both sides of the male / female story." Tamara sighed and caught a tear in her hand as it slipped down her cheek.

"Yes, I am beginning to see why you called me. Not that I questioned your motives. That's why I am here Tamara." He stood up and walked towards her, his eyes softened and a small smile crept across his face as he reached out to comfort and embrace her once more. They stood connected heart to heart in silence breathing in the special moment of union as their aura's blended in harmony, defusing the emotion.

"We don't have much time. You must fill in your application. Come and sit down, I have everything ready for you. I will leave you to survey my choices and then you can make any necessary adjustments." The moment was over as Tamara guided Alistar towards the crystal screen.

"What time do we have to be at the Rose Bowl? I was hoping to catch up with the gang before we have to be seated." Alistar felt her new born excitement and it became infectious. An hour later, Alistar turned to announce "Finished."

"Well, come and have these refreshments. I asked Martha to leave a serve for you. Aren't these cakes darling? I bet they taste great too." Tamara handed him the tiny delicacy and glass of fruit juice.

"Hum! These are super! Special flavour, don't think I have had it before."

They both sat cross-legged on the bed and finished their treats. There was no need for words while they felt their hearts sing in unison. It was a sweet moment of peaceful togetherness. "Now I think we must rest for a few hours, come lay down my sweet."

* * * * *

Meanwhile, Esha had felt restless and decided to take a reflective walk in the Botanical Park, she knew the serenity of the giant trees and the fragrance of the Oleander flowers would centre her focus. As she wandered down the meandering pathways which were lined with deep borders of violets, she breathed deeply. Four pairs of white lace peacocks and a dozen lilac doves heard her soft footsteps and accompanied her.

"Hello my lovelies it's so nice too see you again. Come walk with me." In no time she found herself on the edge of a beautiful sparkling Green lake. Esha was about to sit down by the waters edge and drink in the peace when a familiar voice called out to her.

"Esha! How may I assist you?" It was a whisper, yet not. Esha looked around to try to determine where the voice had emanated from but there was no visible sign to reassure her that the voice was real.

"Esha! How may I assist you?" The call came again but this time there was a vague remembering of this gentle voice, a voice drifting through the ethers from a time in the distant past.

"Is that the Lady of the Lake?" Esha peered into the depths of the emerald waters, searching for the familiar gentle face of the Sacred Feminine.

"Yes, dear one. It is I. You have not forgotten the secrets of Avalon; we can always be together to commune as we practiced during those precious times past. The Goddess energy within you will live on through the ages. Now, more so than ever before, it must resurface into the consciousness on Earth.

Your task for the future life will certainly challenge you, while you nurture and guide women into taking back their power and honour." "Please, tell me more. I have been battling with myself as to whether I should return to our dear Mother Earth in her time of trouble and transition," she lent forward and urgently requested guidance.

"Esha you are a great and wonderful soul, familiar with the Feminine / Goddess and we know you can assist with the Teachings of Healing and Sacred Knowledge." The Lady of the Lake spoke softly with reassurance.

"Yes I can hear what you are saying. Please explain more?" Esha knelt down on the luscious carpet of primroses and listened intently.

"In the times to come much of written history will be exposed as untrue and in your future time, will be rewritten. The Church will be challenged for many conspiracies – as you know the Gospels from Enoch that have been removed from the *good book* and the Magdalene Gospels were spirited away by the Vatican into safe keeping, hiding the truth from prying eyes. Further more, the truth awaits the appropriated time frame to be re-introduced, when the time of freedom dawns. These Gospels will resurface to pay reverence to the equal energy that the Master shared with his Lady." There was a pregnant pause while the Lady of the Lake gave Esha time to digest her message of hope.

"Also the patriarchal attitude to keep women ignorant and under control will begin to fade, as women become more educated and understand the workings of the world, they will start to claim back the power of the Goddess. You, my dear one can be a leader. Can you see the potential of this lifetime?" The Lady of the Lake carefully explained the importance of such an undertaking and the paramount success of this journey. Esha drew in her breath with surprise.

"Oh, I had no idea that this journey could be so powerful in assisting the resurgence of the Goddess energy to the Earth. Now I can see why my heart strings were being pulled. Jacob has asked that we be partners and that in this new lifetime he will be there to support and protect me and that feels good, knowing I can travel with him after so many lifetimes alone." Esha was sounding out her decisions and needed some positive confirmation.

"Yes Esha, you have both worked hard to pass through your initiations. Now you have much knowledge and wisdom to share with women from many countries. Jacob will be your partner in your middle years when you have both completed the former part of your contracts. When you meet it will be for teaching and you will be equal partners in energy and wisdom. Your deep devotion to the mission will always keep you balanced and the foundation of your shared love will be solid as 'the rock,' for together you will complement the Male/Female Principles." "Thank you so much. My heart is now at peace with the future, for I know that I will always be able to connect with the Goddess energy and use the tools I gathered through the Ages." Esha touched her heart and felt the warm wave of love pass through her.

"Esha, there is one more thing I must share." A beautiful sculptured hand rose from the emerald waters and handed her a gift, a small glowing golden Orb.

"Place this near your heart, it will give you strength when times get tough and it will remind you that I am not far away. Remember the Orb also contains the gift of healing and balance for your Spiritual centres. My love goes with you, farewell dear one."

Esha was suddenly alone again, kneeing by the waters edge and she struggled to return to her present reality. As she drifted out of this mystical journey, once more she heard a voice call her name.

"Esha! Where are you? I can feel you close by, please answer." Jacob pleaded from the top of the knoll, visually scanning the park for a sign of her flowing locks.

"Jacob! I am over here by the lake." She waved a greeting to him and then quickly cupped her hand and splashed the sweet water on her face. Just to help her make a dimensional shift back into the garden of reality.

"I have been looking everywhere for you. Are you okay?" He sounded breathless, and as he reached her side he scooped her up in his arms relieved to see her happy face. "You look glowing, what has happened since I saw you last? You seemed so unsure about this journey?" he delivered her to the ground and swung her around in a loop. "Well?"

"Let me catch my breath Jacob." She bent over to touch her toes then straightened slowly up. "I came here to contemplate by myself and when I sat down near the lake I heard a voice calling to me, a very special voice, from ages past!" Jacob became very excited as he gazed into her eyes. "Whom!"

Esha explained her meeting with the Lady of the Lake and the insights she had shared about their future journey.

"Wow! That makes a lot of sense and gives us a much clearer picture of the part we are going to play. No wonder you appear to shine. Let's go tell the others!"

"No, Jacob that information is just for our journey. Each must find their answers for them selves. You know it has always been that way." Esha chided him.

"Yes, you are right. Thank you for sharing what happened to you, I know you didn't have to. Let's hope I remember to respect your talents and intuition when we are on Earth."

"Well Jacob I will be the one to put you in your place. Please come with some sensitivity and recall. Oh, something else. We will meet in our middle years." She stated cautiously.

"Okay! But what comes before that? Do you know?" he questioned her enthusiastically, expecting her to have all the answers.

"No!" Esha teased him and smiled. "What did you put on your application?"

"You know what I put." Jacob replied indignantly with a forlorn face.

"Yes I do but there are always at least two or three potentials that can come to pass. You must remember that from the last journey. Don't worry I will find you, cross my heart. Race you back to the sleeping quarters it must be getting time to meet up with the gang again. They will be wondering where we are." Esha lifted her white gossamer skirt and ran up the hill.

"Wait for me! I wanted to spend this special moment just with the two of us because there won't be another opportunity." Esha stopped in her tracks and waited under a Peppermint tree for Jacob to catch up. He was right; this would be there last precious moments together, with just the two of them. Shortly their friends would call them to join the assembly in the Rose Bowl and then within a short time they would be on their journey. As Jacob reached her side he lifted her chin and looked deep into her eyes then gently touched her mouth with his as they exchanged a tender kiss.

"This will seal our love to the ends of the earth and back. I will find you no matter how far I have to search. We will be together! Hold that in your heart. One day I will see you across a crowded room and we will remember this moment, we will know."

PREPARATION COMPLEX - 9 A.M.

"So, are we all here?" Omha bustled into the room still trying to fix his chef's hat into place. "This is our busy day. Gather around." All the time he was counting heads and tying his apron firmly into place.

"Where is Cherry and Dot?" Omha searched the room for his two most dependable workers. At that very moment the green door flew open and the pair came rushing in giggling and still fixing their uniforms in place.

"We're here Omha! We just went to have a peek at the Rose Bowl. Don't know how they are going to fit all those folk in, don't seem to be that many seats." Dot queried.

"I received a memo informing me that the arrangements will be the same as the orientation program. They will be divided into 'pods', according too their numbered invitation cards. So our plan will be a lot easier to execute, we only have 5,000 folks to deal with at any one time."

"Well that makes this look like a picnic then, shall we begin?" Cherry started to hum one of her favourite melodies and the others joined in. Their hands deftly assembled the Turkish Rolls, wrapping them ready for delivery.

Arthur arrived with a scroll and pinned it to the Notice Board, then announced to one and all. "George and I have built a conveyer belt where you can stack the kebabs on trays ready for the butterflies to collect and deliver."

"What ever do you mean, butterflies to deliver?" asked Matilda with eyes wide open with surprise.

"George and I spent all these weeks trying to devise a plan on how to deliver 5,000 kebabs to all the folks seated at the Rose Bowl. That's a tall order Matilda." His face was serious and then he smiled,

Everyone had downed tools and gave their full attention to Arthur. Now they too were waiting to hear about the butterflies.

"We all know the butterflies here are much larger than on planet Earth. Their colours are breathtaking. Earth butterflies are a much smaller version because of the available food supply. So we considered that our butterflies who have a huge wing span could deliver 50 rolls in one flight." Arthur sounded pleased with himself and he praised George for the part he had played in preparing the plan.

"Wow, that's what I call a plan. So do you want us to stacked 25 rolls on each tray? Just as well we hadn't gone too far down the track. This will make out task much easier. Thank you Arthur."

Matilda walked up to him and gave him a peck on the cheek, smiled and indicated to the others to get a move on, the clock was ticking.

Cherry whispered to Dot, "Won't that look a sight, all those butterflies descending at once into the Rose Bowl. It will appear like Fairyland. Wish we could be there."

"Maybe we will be able to. Cause the work will be finished by then, won't it? If we ask Omha he will probably say 'yes'. What do you reckon, it's worth a try." Dot looked at her friend's face for reassurance and they both nodded, "Come on."

Omha agreed that all the staff had worked extremely well during the past few months and were welcome to watch the butterflies carry out their delivery. This amazing display of nature had never been considered before.

(Butterflies are a metaphysical sign of transformation, due to their four metamorphic stages of growth.)

12
CHAT ROOM

The band of friends had arrived in the vestibule and made their way to the lift. They stood close together and waited in silence.

"Everyone happy with their choices?" asked Liam, looking deeply into their eyes trying to perceive their mood.

"Liam and I will be going to Australia! Won't that be a gas! Never had a lifetime with so much freedom and fun," replied Petra her voice full of excitement. She squeezed Liam's hand tight and gave him a broad smile.

"How about you guys?" The pair asked in unison.

There was a merry banter in the lift, as they compared future lives and ultimately discovered they were all destined to find each other in Australia.

As they alighted from the lift, they heard heated voices coming from the chat room and quickly made steps to discover what the problem was all about. The door lay open and too their surprise Tyler and Isobel were at each other's throats.

"That's not fair, you didn't tell me about that bit!" spat Isobel.

"I know, I know it's my fault for expecting you to go along with it but I thought you would like the challenge." Tyler tried in vain to console Isobel and pleaded with her to hear him out.

"Tyler you know I will agree with most things you suggest and I always have in the past but this is something very different," she lowered her voice and tried miserably to container herself, to be reasonable.

"Isobel sit down and let me explain it to you," he begged her almost on bended knee.

"Okay let me breath for a moment. Don't say a word Tyler. Just let me take five." Isobel walked to the window and gazed out across the emerald lawn which reached as far as the Lake and took three deeps breaths.

The gang stood locked together in the doorway, mystified by the conversation they had just heard, and they still had absolutely no idea what was going on.

"So what is this all about?" queried Petra walking slowly towards Isobel placing a reassuring arm around her shoulder.

The others stood close together holding their breath waiting for a reasonable explanation. They had never heard Tyler and Isobel in dispute, never a cross word had passed between them before. What could have possibly created such a heated scenario?

"Come on in, all of you. My Master volunteered some interesting information about the energy changes that will be taking place during the time frame we will be assisting on Earth." Tyler invited them to be part of the following vision - "The

Goddess energy will be reborn, especially as we draw closer to the new millennium. BUT during the previous years there will be an unfortunate time when this female energy will try to integrate with the masculine energy and this will create great confusion in the physical of many males. It will also disrupt the behaviour of both genders.

You could almost call it a 'cross over' time." Tyler carefully observed their faces wondering if he was making any sense.

"When we are here, we know the true meaning of 'love one another' but when we are in Earth time it is expected that love relationships are between opposite genders." Pause. "The Goddess energy will attempt to soften the masculine energy to assist men to feel with their heart centre. As you know we have all loved one another in different lifetimes but this new process will bring about massive change in attitudes to what love really means, as well as transforming the DNA. How could we possibly explain that to the residents of this coming time?"

The gang sat silent waiting for him to continue, they still could not understand why Isobel and Tyler had displayed such behaviour towards each other. "So what does that have to do with your argument?"

Tyler by-passed the question and continued with his explanation. "During this time frame that we are entering, these people will be known as 'Gays', and have same gender relationships/ marriages. The macho-male will feel threatened and rebel, even if they feel the gentle side of their nature and they will display greater masculine images of being tough. As you know this is how the human persona works to hold on to its identity."

Petra became impatient, "The male DNA energy was set up to protect the female and the community. To build shelter and fight off invaders and that worked well in the past. So are you saying that is going to change?"

Liam butted, "So we all need to remember this conversation, as well as being put on notice that we might feel these changes in our own bodies?"

"I guess that's a good point Liam. And if we are all travelling together as a group of enlightened people we will need to take all this information with us. My reasoning is that we will be in a position to assist women to take back their power. To help them understand that they have a voice. It will also allow us to teach and display more opportunities for equality between the sexes and to change the rules on what is abuse and what is acceptable. That feels like a challenging and worthy lifetime! Don't you think?" Tyler didn't wait for a response and continued with his argument. "After looking into the future, the 'Gay' community which up until this time remained secreted away from prying eyes, and isolated from society and family will start to '*come out*' and because of this they will be ostracized, not permitted in churches, banned from displaying affection in public, targeted by heterosexual males, beaten outside toilets and despised by the public in general." Tyler walked around the table and back again, while the gang sat revetted to their chairs, patiently waiting to hear the remainder of the argument. "Don't we go where Angels fear to Tread, haven't we taken on missions to break through barriers, isn't that what we do?"

"Looking back, I guess you are right. We have done that many times before." Isobel had to agree about their track record.

"And we always put our hands up for the under-dog!" Liam nodded.

"Yes, but . . . this is a bit different." Jacob mused with a long face.

"I hear what you are all saying but there is more. The government of the day will release a laboratory created virus called AIDS, (auto-immune-deficiency-syndrome) which will target third world countries for ethnic cleansing and the 'gay' community." Tyler stopped to monitor their faces and waited for a reaction. Everyone remained silent and took another deep breath, then patiently waited for him to continue. They still had no idea what all the commotion was all about and why did he need to share this information with them anyway!

Joel put his hand up to ask a question, "So what does that have to do with Isobel?"

Tyler hung his head and looked at the floor before replying, then shifted his weight in the chair. The moments passed and they could hear the tick of the clock. He slowly stood up. "Do you remember the many missions we became involved in over the centuries, the Knights Templars, Moses, The Plague in London, French Revolution etc, etc? Well this will be another such mission except this time it's a sexual revolution. It will change the attitude of how people respect our bodies, express their emotions and that 'love has no bounds'. It will bring sex out of survival and procreation into a new light. Over the next 60 years there will be extreme changes in every avenue of Human Consciousness, we cannot even begin to imagine or understand those changes from where we are sitting today. Why are all these changes coming about? Because my dearest friends, it is time for the human race on planet Earth to graduate into responsible, adult, conscious souls. And time to acknowledge that they are creators in their own right, of that third dimensional reality. As the Truth has been withheld by those who deem themselves in authority, such as governments, science and the 'church' we cannot put the full blame on their shoulders. We too have been part of the game through the ages, except we remembered the *'teachings'* and carried them deep within our soul computer. In past times we taught many others who wanted to know and understand these teachings of how the threads of life where woven together. As we step into this new life, it is to assist with the evolution of 'Man', as mankind moves into the next octave of 'Being' a responsible person, a *co-creator*."

The gang remained silent for a few more moments as they tried to absorb the mini lecture, in a very short space of time.

"Yeah! We got most of that when we did the research before submitting our applications. Why did you feel the need to go over that information again?" requested Esha solemnly.

"Because!" Paused and swallowed, then bravely opened his mouth. "I have asked Isobel to become my *'gay lesbian'* lover/ partner, in this coming life. So there it is, now you know why there were words flying when you arrived in the chat-room." Tyler just looked at them not sure of their response.

"Tyler, you must admit that is a big ask! I am sure Isobel will need some time to get her head around such a request. Though we don't really have that sort of time to spare at present," Liam tried to smooth things over for both of them. "It's only a few hours before we have to be at the Rose Bowl. We were coming to get you both."

"Okay, can we help in any way?" volunteered Ruth. "Come on, talk to us. WE have always been there for each other you know you can trust us." This time it was Ruth who moved to place a gentle arm over Isobel's shoulder for comfort.

"It's really alright. I am the one who always looks for the most challenging circumstances and guess what? This time Tyler has surpassed himself. Yes, it came as a shock when he explained what he had volunteered us for. This present scenario has never been presented before, now has it?" Isobel didn't really expect an answer and kept talking. "I have loved Tyler forever and I know he wouldn't ask us to go where it's *too* difficult. But I must admit it does look daunting from this side, God knows what it will be like in the physical condition with all the emotions attached. I hope and pray we have the strength."

She turned to Tyler and threw him a serious question. "Are you saying love will find a way?" But Tyler didn't have time to reply when Jacob cut in to acknowledge their courage.

"Well I think you guys are really brave to travel into this unknown chaos, taking on new and unexplored identities. We acknowledge that this is not something new, these relationships have occurred throughout history. Now you are saying that it may become more common amongst society. We wish you luck, all of us."

"I am glad it's not me. Now you have put us on notice, we will need to be more compassionate towards folk who are different. What am I saying? Just listen to me? Folks who are different!" Ruth questioned herself for the first time. Suddenly it became very clear that this future life was going to be challenging, as never before.

"We are going as gay women, to empower the Goddess energy. That is if Isobel will agree." Tyler stated proudly and watched their faces change.

"And you will succeed very well." They replied in unison. "And we will always love you both, no matter what."

CRYSTAL DOME

Now, can you guess who gathered on this auspicious day? Earth was once more moving through a Dark Age, yet it remained unaware of the necessary preparation for massive change, yet to come. It would take many brave, forward thinking souls to drag the spiritual energy into the new millennium and prevent annihilation. For at this present time all humans were running on the sacrificial energy of the Piscesian Age.

I ask you, "Who heralded in the Piscesian Age with the greatest sacrifice? And who delivered the Bread and the Wine? Yes, thousands of followers had all partaken of these rituals for two thousand years. Acknowledging and reinforcing the practice of the Christ energy (the energy of sacrifice.) Now as the century draws to a close, there must come radical CHANGE and awakening to progress into the Aquarian Age."

The **Master of Ceremonies** stepped up to the rostrum and raised his arms in salutation and waited for the hush to descend.

"Now I would like to introduce you to the Ascended Masters, the Guardians of this Galaxy; The Time Lords and the Keepers of Wisdom. These Beloved Ones are familiar to each and every one of you, as teacher, friend and advisor. You have sat before them or cried on their shoulder during different segments and phases of your Soul journey. Now they come to speak to you as a collective consciousness, in honour and reverence to those who sit before us in this moment of time. You, dear ones who have chosen to play an extremely demanding role in the immediate years to come. Please welcome our Ancient Ones…"

The lights came up as the Ancient Ones filed onto the dais, centre stage. Each dressed in the radiant colours of their station. They bowed in honour to the audience.

"Welcome to our Speakers. At 2 o'clock we will pause to provide you with refreshments. Then we will continue until all the relevant information has been disseminated. There will also be time for questions.

Dear Peacemakers, you are to be congratulated for your love of Mankind. For recognising the wonderful qualities of the Divine Spirit in Man and the turbulent journey they are walking. Your task will not be easy, remember we will guide your footsteps each part of the way." He turned and acknowledged those seated on the platform.

"The Earth Planet has been set up with many varied precious stones to keep the optimum balance. In the future you will access these energies to assist in the healing field, also to expand the human mind into opening doorways of locked memories that up until now have remained dormant in the recesses of the mind. Since the time of Atlantis when the Crystal Energy was used for power and greed, the technology has been hidden.

You will witness Nature in her splendour, as she heightens your energy fields with magnificent colours and visions of God's grace. These will be given to you as signs, which you will remember from this moment when we gathered on this day. Walk with the trees and bathe in the oceans to renew and cleanse your own energy fields. Meditate on your own Divine Spirit. Seek like minded people who will relate to your journey and offer support." Pause.

"Recall some of the old ways of healing and introduce them as complimentary Natural Medicine, for they are found in the Plant Kingdom, and they are in tune with the physical meridians and have been administered by many of our healers through the ages. That is why they were placed on the earth as such."

The Master closed his eyes and took three deep breaths, while the audience sat respectfully waiting in anticipation for the next revelation.

"The Crystal Kingdom is prepared to surface for your work to take place. Many millennia have past since they assisted mankind, for they remember the abuse that was wrought on their Kingdom. Now, after many centuries of cleansing they are prepared to rise to the surface once again and be counted as part of the collective once more, to bring balance and healing. Respect their choices to aid you. Learn their individual qualities, honour their beauty. Teach yourselves to hear and feel their language. Tune into their energy for healing and cleansing the physical body and when their work is done, return them to the good earth. This is their natural homeland."

There was another quiet pause, as the Master skilfully surveyed the radiant faces of the future Earth Angels seated before him.

"And now I will introduce my first speaker to you. One you all know very well. The Masters of The Crimson Circle stand before the large gathering. Each one will address the overwhelming problems that are taking place on Earth Planet at that very moment."

The grand crowd of 144,000 waited intently for the progressive assignments that were about to be presented, which will challenge them on all levels of mastery.

"You have ALL heard my words from a long time ago. Once before, many eons ago we gathered just like this on the hills of Jerusalem, your souls have not forgotten the message of Love and Compassion. The message has not changed. Those who sit here today have breathed and lived this message in many life times and have remembered the price of persecution, they paid. Once more you will be put to the test of following your hearts desire, to teach those who have not grasped my concepts –

'That we are all one.'

As the new millennium approaches the 'Christ Consciousness' will filter through the ethers to assist you. We, the ANGELS and MASTERS will watch over you and support your brave efforts. Do not forget that we are close at hand, only a thought away, sitting in a different dimensional space ready to guide you through the tough days that lie ahead." Lights of rainbow colours flashed, imbuing each participant with strength and courage. Yeshua continued, "You are the Peacemakers, the new Pioneers for the Aquarian Age and we must send you forth to make preparation. Our hearts are sad that you must leave us for a time.

Your journey will be a lonely one, hold on to the knowingness that you are dearly loved." Tears welled up and spilled over, Yeshua recalled the pain of the human journey and his compassion went out to every volunteer.

"We will hide you like needles in a haystack until the appointed time. To protect you from those who may harm you. Your talents will be far superior; telepathy, sensitivity and knowingness of the truth, which could open you to ridicule. When you come of age and have found your strengths disguised as stubbornness, steadfastness and rebellion, only then will you be strong enough to stand up for your beliefs and communicate the changes you collectively will bring about. Do not falter. You have a monumental task to achieve. Use compassion in all your dealings with others. Care for the sick and elderly. Do not continue to walk in sacrifice. Those days are coming to a close. As the millennium approaches find the 'key'. Know that you are dearly loved for the work you are doing.

There will be those of you who will be, the teachers of the day, and have the ability to channel guidance from our realms, where the Master's will assist you with Universal wisdom. Wherever possible, we will be at your service to give you knowledge and understandings of the imminent changes taking place. Will you commit to be the teachers for the coming days, for the new energy?"

"Yes, we will be the teachers!" sounded the jubilant chorus in reply.

"Now we shall drink with you, raise your Cup of Celestial Wine to celebrate this Divine gathering of the Peacemakers. May Love and Light guide your footsteps until you return here to dwell with US once more?" Yeshua touched his heart and bowed his head, then stood with His arms outstretched in a salute – "Blessings my Beloved Ones until we meet again."

MASTER BUDDHA

Stepped forward and bowed to the congregation with deep respect.

"For too long the East and West have been divided over their spiritual practices, yet the basic teachings are of the same truth. Not realising that the coin has two faces, two sides that are equally important, neither side shines brighter than the other. Yet, together their value is a hundred times greater. During the moment of prayer, whilst on bended knee, the focus is that you are smaller and in need. Therefore the *prayer* is to ask to be greater. Now, we ask that you use prayer for *'thanks, gratitude, protection and abundance'*. Meditation is practiced for seeking the inner knowledge that is stored within your soul memory for reference and guidance on this journey. Please combine the two practices to gain a greater understanding of how they fit together for your wellbeing. With this understanding you go forward into this Mercy mission with your hearts full of Love and Compassion to herald in change and expansion for the planet Earth?" Master Buddha lifted his arms in praise to the congregation.

The chorus rang out in unison and joy, ***"Yes, we do!"***

"Some may still use the practice of living within the safety of monastery walls to stay focused on their inner rituals of service to the Divine. Planet Earth is in great need of these peaceful sanctuaries. While many of you will take up a greater challenge to live an ordinary life, with family, friends and careers. This will also allow you to take up studies in Alternative Thinking and Medical Practices. Encouraging folks to open their minds in a structured society and take back their power of choice. Giving a greater number of folk the opportunity to move into alternative remedies and become attuned to their deeper wisdom, to understand how the mind/body is joined in the perfection of physical well-being. So, WE salute you! To you the Peacemakers and Pathfinders of the future years to come, we thank you. You will forge a new millennium with advanced knowledge and introduce meditation, astrology and techniques of self-healing. For you will be judged as wacky, fruit-loops and off-the-planet. In your heart of hearts you will remember what was spoken of on this most momentous occasion, and you heart will hear the tune that resonates to your inner truth. We will watch over you and guide your footsteps as you take up this challenge to assist Peace on this planet." He picked up his Cup and held it high.

"Now we shall drink from the Cup of Celestial Wine to celebrate this Divine gathering of the Peacemakers."

Twice now, the audience had raised their Cup to seal their pledge. The infectious energy encouraged the crowd, their Spirits soared as the message of Faith, Hope, and Love gave impetus to the mission.

Not all the gatherers were ready to sacrifice their future missions for the upgraded genesis and some had quietly slipped away. The numbers had dwindled. None were judged for their choices, for they had walked in their Truth and remained passionate to their future plan.

ST FRANCIS walked to the rostrum and quietly faced the audience.

"Beloved friends, in the past your animals were the workers on the land and guardians of Temples and Monasteries. Quiet servants of truth and prepared to supply much of your sustenance. Many creatures still transport loads of wood, sacks of grain and rice, for exchange at the markets. Yes, there will always be those who continue their original tasks....if you treat them well. This is a warning for future practices of farming. Be vigilant about the foods your creatures ingest, for there may not always be an abundant supply of pasture. You will witness climate changes that maybe natural or scientifically controlled, there will be a great need to prepare and store extra feed and grain. Remember the old ways – when there is a bountiful harvest, it is telling you to prepare for the year of famine. Collect and store, fresh water for times of drought. Be aware of artificial ingredients.

Your pets will be co-workers, ready to share your burdens and relieve your dis-eases. Treat them with respect for you are their guardians, they are your divine friends in disguise, ready to serve your needs and comfort your hearts in troubled times.

When the years are void of travelling companions, your pets will warm the empty spaces and afford you the opportunity to open your heart, to embrace pure love. Learn how it feels for they have no agenda or judgement. Many of you will take an active part in protecting endangered species, the ones who are being slaughtered for clothing and ancient medicine.

Many of your animals will leave planet Earth as they have fulfilled their evolution and their natural habitat has disappeared or been polluted by toxic waste or greed. Allow them the dignity of departure. Do not attempt to constrain them in small holding pens for folks to gape at in wonder. Respect the living process of Nature.

Teach the children of the future to love and cherish pets. As your world becomes clogged with suburbia there will not be the open spaces for children to enjoy interaction with creatures that once would have been part of their daily ritual.

Some of you will build Rescue Havens for the abandoned creatures which are left at rubbish tips, on verges of highways when very young, very old, maimed or simply unwanted.

You will be greatly needed in the years to come, to hold the value and love connection of so many creatures that fill your lives, for they will bring you great joy. Remember they are an extension of your energy and love.

We Bless You.

This will show you the way to Unconditional Love and Love of Self, for the animal kingdom is a part of you. Remember WE are all ONE. SO, gentle souls we raise our glass to you and drink from the Cup of Celestial Wine to give you courage.

QUAN YIN – Feminine Energy

"My energy will become more accessible in the years to come. At present this Earth world operates within the masculine energy. The governments of the day still use their power to manipulate and control the populace through fear. The ying-yang symbol will trigger the memory of this day as we gathered to find solutions to bringing about balance. This Eastern symbol needs to reach, Western minds. In time there will be a melding of philosophies as the two forge a balance within the body, mind and soul. This new energy will encourage each one of you, to look to your inner worlds, to learn to love and nurture the self. **Love comes from within**. When you each learn to care and love the true self you will not need to ask another to love you and appreciate who you are. When this is achieved you will remember this moment when you sat in this chair and volunteered to take this awesome journey to bring about change. Planet Earth as been on an extensive learning curve to reach maturity, we have been ever watchful of the progress. It is now time to blend the energies and become one with the self. As present day relationships dissolve and become a thing of the past, we will assist you to find more harmonious unions. Relationships will be with balance and responsibility where you travel on equal roads, each playing your true part as whole being, sharing a life together. There will be resistance to these changes, especially in the masculine world, the business world and in the churches. Change always brings resistance.

Women will have to be strong and stick to their principles. Raise children, free of abuse. Take on a double role of protection as men adjust their energies into more nurturing modes. Those of you who choose a feminine role will have to be prepared with extra skills to survive this drastic time of change. We will enhance your energy with stamina to withstand the stormy tides of domestic change. Cultural change brings unrest and drama, you will be able to access your collective knowledge and bring it to the fore as spiritual intuition. Have empathy but do not collapse into the romantic, love space, we ask you to use 'tough love' as a survival tool. Combine this with compassion as you observe the inner struggle.

For the one's who will choose to be male gender, you will feel a gentleness come from within and many will not understand the *feeling*. Do not misinterpret this change in the DNA, for it shall affect all humans, as they move towards the new energy of 2000.

We will take a break to stretch our legs. Discuss amongst your fellow companions, the information that has been implanted thus far. We shall assemble again in two hours time. To take a count of the brave, courageous, worthy souls who return to their seats.

Thank you for hearing our call. We send blessings to each one of you."

TIME OUT

The gang huddled together in a small corner, ducking for cover from the immense crowd as they moved quickly to open ground. Each volunteer deep in thought about the coming events and the outstanding information they had just received. They had been offered a short time to review their decision to return to the Earth Planet. Were they ready? Were they prepared?

"So what do you think?"

"I really don't know?"

"Maybe this is going to be too..Oo. Hard?"

"Are we going back to hear the remainder of the talk?"

"I don't know if I'm ready."

"Stop that negative talk right now!" Alistar cut in, irritated with the chatter. "You were all full of excitement and passion a few hours ago. We didn't come together and map out the new mission just to chicken out. We all felt the call; don't you think that stands for something?" He stood firm with his hands on his hips, a look of disbelief masked his disappointment.

They all fell silent with shameful looks on their faces waiting to see who would take courage to reply first.

"Let's get outside in the fresh air and breathe a little before any of you say another word. Come on, we don't have a lot of time to discuss this."

The group sat quietly, on the soft lawn and waited for the first person to offer guidance. It was Jacob who spoke first, "We were so committed just a few hours ago. We couldn't wait to get started on this new adventure, so what has changed? Who got spooked? Come on speak up!"

Esha and Petra owned up, "We felt uncertain about our ability to be strong enough to be of any assistance to the group." And pair hung their heads in shame. "We know how much we love each other but will that be enough?"

"Of course it will be enough. We have pledged to be there for each other, maybe in different guises but we will be there. The group energy will flow, we will find each other. Come on we proofed that yesterday when we first arrived here, with all these people we still arrived at the same spot, how good is that?" Liam put his view forward and nodded.

"Yes but you don't understand! It's so much more challenging if we go as women. We won't have the opportunities that men have, so how will we be able to assist in the teachings?" Petra raised her eyebrows and waited for an intelligent reply.

"Women are responsible as Mothers to teach their sons to be more tolerant towards the female gender. That is very important, don't you think? You can make a huge difference to male attitudes and teach them to respect women's feelings and biology." Alistar threw the question as a challenge.

"I guess you're right." Esha backed down and chewed on her lip thoughtfully before ushering her next question.

Tyler butted in and requested, "So are there any more queries or hesitations that we should discuss at this point in time? Or are we, what?"

"What do you mean are we what?"

"There's no what about it. I'm sure we will be reassured and the Master's will not let us venture forth without sufficient information to get us through this journey. We must have enough confidence in our own ability to achieve all we sent out to do. Think positive. Come on folks, we can do this. Especially as we are going together!" Alistar reassured them.

Joel stood up and announced, "We have already decided and I think we should stick to our plans. Apart from all this nonsense, we haven't heard the remainder of the information yet."

Ruth stood beside him and declared, "Come on get up, we must stick together and it's time to take our seats again. Come on, it will be exciting!"

"Okay, let's go."

The group scrambled to their feet and ran back to the Crystal Dome.

MASTER KYRON - The Magnetic Master of Gaia

"We welcome each and every one of you who has taken up the call to return at this critical time of Earth's evolution, for you are brave souls who march to a different tune. This lifetime will bring many challenges. We salute you.

As you approach the 'end times' you will burst out of your silent cocoons and reveal the 'truth'. You will have reached your goal and communicate your 'true selves.' The years of silence will have been necessary to collect the hidden information concerning the original beginnings. There was an agenda that was put into place many thousands of years earlier to govern and control the masses. Now as we approach the new millennium, (while many of you will reach this age of maturity, some will find the going too tough and return to us and we will celebrate your journey) it will be time to reveal the program and transcend into the freedom of your true 'spiritual nature'. I, KYRON the Magnetic Master will guide you through with channelled information and you will remember my words on that day.

Your power to communicate will be aided by an advanced technology, unknown at this present time on Earth. A network of unity will become available. This will be a great learning curve that you are all capable of mastering. A *master tool* to connect and strengthen your mission! Oh there will be wondrous times of awakening but this will be off-set by much unrest as the multitude come to realize the fog of illusion that has been placed on their belief systems and that they have been walking in a dark cloud of manipulation. Communication and truth will ask them to become flexible enough to change their thinking patterns, to let go of their crutches of *religion and slave hood* to become adult beings with the power to master their own journey into Enlightenment.

For that is what these times are all about, the 'End Times' of illusion. Asking the people of Earth to mature as Spiritual Beings and take up their power as we move closer towards the 21st century.

There is much information written in the old texts, on ancient scrolls and carved in stone that will enlighten the scholars of the day. This information has been hidden and secreted away by those in control / power. There will come a day when this will be released by the very people that sit before me. For you have experienced many lifetimes on this planet and will also have gained entry to the Akashic Records. We will guide you to this information as necessary in your dream state, to bring forth the truth.

As Gaia passes through the Photon Belt she will be preparing for her own ascension into the 5th dimension, heralding in the Golden Age.

As you all mature, along with your planet there will be many changes. Free the mind of restrictions, become like the young sapling, *be flexible* or you will break under the weight of rigidity, otherwise you will not survive the storms of economic, religious, moral, racial and geographic change.

These will be exciting times my friends, times when *change* has never been more radical and extensive. Times of gigantic change as we ALL prepare for transition.

You will be the Lighthouses during this powerful transition. Stand tall. Blessings to each and every one of you.

I AM KYRON the Magnetic Master

SAINT GERMAIN - MASTER of the VIOLET FLAME

"I AM, Saint GERMAIN. I am the convener of the Forces of Light. You are part of a vast collective, a colossal display of demonstrated mastery. You are a fundamental stitch in the fabric of evolution. We are a family of *light*. You are part of that same vibration whether you are sitting before us or whether you are incarnate. When you take on physical form you may not see those who stand beside you, it will be family who guide your footsteps through the next crucial phase of evolvement. **There will be an untold changement for all of the emerging masters in your earth realm. It is a time of great acceleration and the changes** that come to you will be unfathomable. They will certainly be new, or appear to be new to you all. Yet you are well prepared; you have all passed through the mystery schools and mastery schools of the eons. Within you, you carry the wisdom of the ages in readiness for the time to come. Self-acceptance, and honouring self – will be the greatest tool and one that shall open doors for your future life. We ask that you liberate yours selves from a sense of limitation to find the truth of yourself: The truth of your greatness, the truth of your absolute sovereignty over each and every moment of your reality. As you open your hearts and your minds to the potential of this, it will become increasingly active and influential in your lives. It will be vital that you begin to allow the evolution of your personal truth, rather than to see truth as being something that is static, or a known quantity.

What you choose to believe is true will become true for you. We will encourage you to reconstruct the belief system that has been laid down in your younger years.

You will be the generation of 'Way Showers' the ones who will lay the Path for those yet to come. You will break through the barriers of belief patterns that have kept humanity in bondage for so long. Their Hearts have been made heavy with restrictions of guilt, shame and fear. There has been little room for Unconditional Love. We will guide you into a new era of *open hearts* where you will feel and express your inner joy of life. Where you will demonstrate your free will to be your true selves; the loving spirit within. There will be many new tools presented to you such as:

music, media and literature to aid the release of knowledge. You are all experts in your own field. I, Saint Germain will guide your footsteps to assure this knowledge is presented at each specific stage of your learning. The first step will be to understand the power of the Violet Flame and the cleansing properties for the physical, emotional and mental bodies. This will enlighten your senses and release past and present problems in the physical. This shall also assist Gaia and aid Her Ascension into the next phase of enlightenment. You have chosen a life of *service* for the greater plan for the greater good of ALL. We salute you. Oh! Brave Warriors of Light.

Let's all breath in the Violet Flame to give you strength and courage before you begin this awesome journey. Will you pledge to remember my words?"

"YES, we will follow your guidance and remember your wisdom!"

"One day, in the not so distant future I will remind you of this day and in that future time frame I will present to you, 'The Five Secret Rays' they will become available for your personal use and advancement. Then at a later date, having mastered that energy you will step forward and teach the qualities of Initiation to your students. "

The **Master of Ceremonies** stepped up to the rostrum and raised his arms in salutation.

"Now just before we take a breather and receive nourishment, I have a few chosen words.   We have a grand surprise for you.

The audience became aware of a gentle 'hum', ALL looked up to observe the roof of the crystal dome opening to reveal a soft pink sky.

"In a few moments you will have a Celestial Banquet delivered to you. We have spent many weeks preparing this grand feast. As you already know, the butterflies in this realm are so much bigger and brighter in colour than on Earth. Their wing span is 10 feet across, and they can transport many packets of sustenance. Please wait for their grand entrance."

A moment later the butterflies came into view.

"Wow look at that!"

All eyes were raised to the opening, to witness the grand entrance of the butterflies. Each participant greeted their personal butterfly.

"After your meal we will continue."

The Masters moved to the centre of the dais, joined hands as it descended to a lower floor beneath the stage.

A soft modulated voice informed, "Press the blue button on the back of the seat in front of you. There you will find a unique cavity which will dispense sweet juice, soft tissues with cologne and a chocolate bar. Enjoy the feast. Blessings on this grand gathering.

"I wouldn't miss this for the world. They are so beautiful!" Isobel whispered and squeezed Liam's hand.

GAIA – MOTHER EARTH FEMININE, NURTURER
(a vision appeared on the holographic template)
Revealing the beautiful essence of Mother Earth

"Welcome my sweet, brave EARTH INHABITANTS to be, those who are ready to return once more on this journey of *service to spirit*. We have endeavoured to prepare you with facts for your forthcoming adventure. All will not be pretty in the years to come as you witness many changes. Changes which will stir your passion as the greedy invade my shores, pollute my oceans and rape my lands. Are you ready to take up my cause?"

The gathering rose to their feet and chanted, *"Yes we are!"*

"I thank you for your courage. Your devotion to the Blue Planet brings tears of joy to my eyes. For Earth is a magnificent creation. One in which you have all played a part.

This is why we must prepare you for the future potentials. Many countries now move into an industrial era which will encourage great wealth and material gain. Unfortunately this will also bring substances which will harm my ecological balance. Extreme pollution will damage my oceans with mercury and biological fallout, ones that are not present on the earth at this time. Many new minerals will be discovered and my lands will be raped of precious metals that keep the meridians equalized. Future energy sources will be abused and turned into weapons of destruction; which in turn will invade the stratosphere and produce ozone holes and subtle particles, thus creating many health issues. Maybe, even the temperatures around the globe will change drastically and create massive weather pattern changes unseen on this planet before. I will have my work cut out to keep the balance and maybe I too will have to make some earth changes to adjust and cleanse the work of **Man.**

Your early years will provide you with natural food to sustain your young forming biological body. This will give you a strong immune system to combat the coming revolution in the food chain. We are not trying to put you off this journey but you do need to know this information before you commit to your final decision in the hours to come. We ask that you take this away with you to contemplate the serious implications of this adventure.

Having given you many of the negatives, I will now introduce you to some of the positive out looks.

- Much improved health conditions and medical practices
- Higher Education for women
- Science will expand the boarders of the space frontier.
- Improved living conditions
- Medicine will discover the structure of 'life'
- Industry will expand with new design
- Women will be able to hold bank accounts and jobs
- Communication will increase in all areas
- Freedom of speech
- Technology will blow your mind away

- There will be a SPIRITUAL Revolution which you will birth.
- The Truth of humanity will be revealed.
- Mankind will reach the age maturity
- And many more surprises that at present you can only dream about.

We cannot tell you ALL, for it will depend on you to create the new programs. Your passion will alert you to the timely changes, as you reach into your heart for answers.

I will feel you and know you as you walk gently on the Earth. As you honour my forests, lakes and seashores, we will commune.

Bathe in my oceans. Watch the night skies. Herald in the solstice, protect the creatures of the deep and Celebrate my seasons.

There is much to achieve this time around. Ponder on my words of warning Blessed Ones of courage, for you are truly loved for your Service.

Take with you ALL the wisdom you have gathered over your many incarnations for you will find it necessary to access this in times of stress and uncertainty.

In time you will find one another and pool your information. You will support each other when you feel at a loss or alone. Gather together your collective knowledge and teach those who are willing to change. Show them by example that numbers have strength and power.

You will revise the old Essene / Pagan ways of honouring the Living Spaceship that you travel on – ways to keep the Gaia essence replenished. **You will be our Earth Angels**.

We the WATCHERS and GUIDES will work with you every step of the way. Together we are an awesome team. You will lay new foundations for the coming Millennium. Many times you will question, 'What are the ultimate steps we need to take to move the planet forward but we assure you, you will be guided.'

Remember you are not alone. We the Collective salute you and Bless You.

TOBIAS - Master TEACHER

"So we have explored all the positive outlooks of your future journey. It all sounds very rewarding and exciting. You are going to bring about much transformation. It is my duty to put before you some of the *not so* glamorous conditions of this lifetime.

Now I AM here to remind you of the negatives that are possibilities, you could call it a reality check. All these must be considered carefully before embarking on this mission.

Change is a natural state of the nature and the universe, we all understand this law. During this life-span we are talking about accelerated change as never before on planet Earth, that is connected to basic structure of family, morals, culture, finances, workplace and religion.

I will allow you to contemplate what I have just proposed."

A silence fell over the congregation. Our friends looked at each other but dared not speak while the master looked deep into the soul of each one seated in front of him.

And HE waited.

"You are ALL the Divine Heart of GOD. We are asking you to go forth and awaken the hearts and minds of MAN to this revelation."

Once more HE waited for the realization of this statement to sink into each and everyone who was present.

"Are you prepared to be ridiculed and persecuted for your forward thinking and teachings? Life will be a challenge! For you will be asking folks to surrender their belief systems, their very foundations. Not an easy task, dear ones. These are their crutches and while it is so they cannot come to know their true selves, that they are also a spark of the Divine. They will continue to live in the shadow of a fearful God, always asking for guidance and forgiveness. While the Church holds them to ransom, to purchase a ticket *to heaven, the people only fill their coffers for their own power and glory.* Are you ready to challenge the Churches! Think about that for a moment."

The silence grew heavy.

"You will also challenge the medical profession with new ways of dealing with *self healing*. When I say *new ways* that is not totally true because many of these new ways are *old practices* which need to be restored and **combined** will modern medicine. You will be the ones who take up the art of these new ways and start

115

introducing these practices until they are accepted as a permanent structure of the healing mode. Yes! You will be challenged and sabotaged for many years but you will be triumphant.

For those who choose to move into the art of Meditation, you will be ridiculed. The majority will not be able to see this as a form of prayer, gratitude and thanksgiving. Nor will they relate this to a form of self-healing and forgiveness. During these coming years the East and the West will merge with a new understanding that they are ONE."

THE GATHERING nodded their heads in silence, listening intently to every word from the Master.

"Strict moral judgment will change. Those who are locked into unsatisfactory marriages will now find the law assisting them to revoke their vows and be released to find happiness with another partner. Even against the unrelenting pressure of the church. Many of you will find yourselves in this position and it will bring you much grief and disappointment. But I ask you to remember that once LOVE has connected IT can never be undone or destroyed. The human condition will feel the pain and try to master its emotions, but the Soul will recall my words of warning and continue its journey. While you are walking the Earthly Life you will also be following your contract. The contract that you will agree too, before you leave this place. Please remember that at the same time you will be balancing your Karmic destiny with those you choose to travel with. Those from the past and the present; those who will also be present in the future. Leave NO stone unturned in this area for it will touch the matrix and ripple throughout the universe of every tomorrow. Love is the answer."

Tobias, stood tall and proud as he surveyed the brave souls sitting in the chairs before him.

"I AM not here to be the bearer of ill fortune. I AM here to inform you of what you are preparing to take on during this coming lifetime of challenge. Pilgrims of Peace, you will need every ounce of courage and yet it will be exciting and rewarding as you forge new ground. It will stretch you to your limits. It will expand your creativeness. It will touch your soul to the breath, length and depth of Who You Are but you are very capable of this challenge. We the **Masters** must prepare you with ALL the information necessary, it is our duty.

Now, having conveyed this, I will also inform you that WE the Masters will be available to guide and teach you throughout this time of transformation. We want to reassure you that we will not leave you to tread this journey *alone*. Your psyche will be heightened and your link to US in these other dimensions will hold a strong connection. You may feel that you have lost touch with your mission but that will not be so.

As you move closer to each Astrological window of Change we will remind you. There will also be critical times when you will be asked to open Portals of Energy. There will be times of Great Transformation. Gateways for collective Celebration. Comets, to seed new ideas and technology. They will be very exciting times. As these events come to pass WE will be there with you. WE will celebrate with you and share your excitement, egg you on, so to speak. When the pathway gets too tough, WE will stand beside you. WE will share your tears and your joys. Reach out to US. Ask for a guiding light, a sign, and WE will respond."

Tobias stopped for a moment and wiped a tear from his eye.

"You will never be alone. Before you leave *to fly through the wind of birth*, you will also make a contract with those 'beloved ones' who are family, those who will watch over you and walk by your side from this dimension. You will be dearly loved.

AND when it is TIME, you will hear my voice again to give you direction and knowledge for the NOW moment. I will remind you of the time we sat here and discussed these matters and I will love you through those TIMES as we approach the END DAYS together."

Tobias stood still and took three deep breaths before continuing.

"And when you return to the Halls of Honour we will celebrate the magnificent changes that took place during your lifetime while you were away from US. We will drink a glass of wine and share your adventure with all those, as they return. For we know you will not stay with us for very long, before you travel forward to a new experience. Just enough time to relay the wonders and magnificence of your creation.

Blessed are the Peace Makers and the Pioneers who go forth to create this magnificent Transformation."

MASTER KUTHUMI

"And So It Is, Beloved Ones! Are you ready?" Kuthumi looked deep into their souls and smiled to himself. "Hum!"

The dedicated ones who were present waited patiently while He surveyed their reaction to His quiet inspection. There was no judgment, only love and admiration shone from his eyes.

"During your progressive stay, as you mature in daily wisdom and collective knowledge we will assist you to open and access charkas that until this time in evolution have remained closed. Only a select few have managed to achieve this energy through patience and solitude within the walls of a chosen monastic discipline."

Once more He paused, contemplating His next words.

"As these physical portals are activated it will allow you to access higher vibrations of energy and knowledge. To balance and self heal from life's emotional traumas. At specific mile stones in your growth we will assist you and information will be presented to you through your guardians and spiritual teachers."

Inwardly He decided this was enough information to carry them through.

"You dear ones, will be tested for your tenacity, strength and compassion. We the Council have faith in your integrity to complete your journey. But.......... if, you find the going tooo tough, heartbreaking, or soul destroying because of the energy and changes in social structure, we say to you in this moment. 'It is acceptable for you to return HOME.' As we can foresee the many difficulties you will encounter, we do not wish to discuss the negative influences that you may encounter in the next 50 years. We only need to point out there will be huge challenges, even for you, our chosen ones. You will each carry what is called a 'starseed' and this will allow you to recognize each other when the time is right for you to become a collective."

Kuthumi paused and looked into the distance, trying to put together comforting reassurance for the travellers that sat before him in silence.

"You are our brave Warriors of Light. There are special teachers that have already been placed at your disposal, the Ones that went before you to lay the foundation of knowledge. Knowledge, which will find its way to you in the most unexpected way. Some of these respected avatars of wisdom will shortly return to US, as their job has been completed. What you need to find will be in script, look for the unexpected journals of these for-runners and bless their diligence and skill. Blessings to you ALL, our love and adoration go with you to keep you safe until you return."

ARCHANGEL   RAPHAEL

"Although this is a solemn day, it is also a most joyful day! A day of celebration, when we celebrate your courage and fortitude! We the Collective Council thank you with open hearts. This journey will test your belief in yourselves and your collective knowledge because when you pass through the *veil of forgetfulness* you may feel lost and forgotten. We ask you to enjoy a rightful and joyous childhood which will provide a sound physical immune system and the ability to laugh with yourself."

Archangel Raphael paused with a smile on His face waiting for a reaction.

"As children you will be able to communicate with your *spirit friends* and share a different world with them, you may find you are left to your own devices with nature. This will afford you respite from the outer world around you which may feel harsh and uncomfortable. During those times we will be close by watching over our charges. You will come to know you are never alone, even if you cannot share this with your parents."

Archangel Raphael allowed this information to sink into the conscious mind, as each one present felt the impact. The seed had been sown in the soul for remembering.

"We the keepers of the elements will teach you to be sensitive to magnetic changes, energy changes. This will alert you to nature's forces as a protection. In times to come this will be a valuable asset, for there will be many *earth changes* during your lifetime and you will become familiar with these energy changes on short notice. You will be familiar with the seasons of the SUN, be fascinated with the march of the stars across the heavens, rejoice with the wind on your face and bathe in the waters of the ocean. All this will have meaning for you. And you will wonder why and yet it will all feel so comfortable and natural. Why?

Because you will know you are a part of Gaia. You will always respect the space ship you are travelling on and understand the fine balance of nature. Part of your mission will be to bring about harmony, to keep the balance and respect all the diverse creatures and numerous *races* that travel by your side.

Many species will be abused, unnecessarily and you will become part of a World Wide program to preserve and protect those creatures from extinction. Does it sound like a tall order that we are presenting to you? Well it is! Are you ready?

God speed, to each and every one of you. Always be your true God self. Know you are truly loved." He bowed to the audience and returned to his seat of office.

DALI LAMA

"It is a proud and precious moment that brings me to this gathering. A great gathering of so many brave enlightened souls who are prepared to step forward once again and be counted. Each one of you has sat before me at some moment in time to learn the art of solitude and service to mankind. You have acquired the peace within, even though it may have been fleeting while in physical form.

It is only now that you understand that the lifetimes of discipline were only a preparation for all the future lifetimes yet to come. Now is that time. A predicted time, as we approach the *end times* as foretold in the Mayan Calendar. For the Ancient Ones were versed with the progression of Time and Evolution and conscious of this grand event yet to come.

You may wonder why this information has been secreted away from the masses. Why has this not been public knowledge? Many indigenous cultures secreted this knowledge from amongst their tribal story-tellers. The Wise Ones knew there would come a time when they would be asked to come forward to enlighten the majority, even at the risk of their lives."

The Dali Lama moved forward and drank from a glass of water and cleared His throat.

"We, the Tibetans have held this knowledge for many generations. Deep within the walls of our monasteries lie the scrolls and teaching from the *beginnings of time*. Knowledge that needed to be in safe keeping until the *time* was right for it to be revealed. Our high Initiates have been instructed in the awareness of these teachings. We were not the only ones who protected this knowledge. As you are aware the Astez and many South American tribes were also caretakers, aware that the 'Manipulators' wished to keep the progressive knowledge of evolution to themselves."

He stopped and looked around the sea of faces that were tuned to His every word and smiled, his face lighting up with passion.

"You too will become the caretakers and discover the Truth. You will be the ones who seek the truth, write the books and sometimes find your life threatened. Your desire to share your findings will be your passion! Sometime in the future you will find yourselves making journeys to distant lands because your heart will pull you to follow your personal mission. A door will open in your memory, of the day you sat in these chairs and heard my words. And you will be right on track. Don't let anyone talk you out of the adventure.

By this time you will know that I reside on Earth, you will see my face, hear my words and you may even sit before me in an audience. Your heart will sing with resonance. I will smile, bow my head and acknowledge your presence. And I will know you, each one of you and we will feel that connection.

Blessings to each of you, for one day we will gather again here and we will speak of the 'Day of Ascension'. The day is yet to come when the Earth Planet will be welcomed into the family of the Galactic Federation."

MASTER SANANDA - Lord and Guardian of Earth

"For hundreds of years I have watched thousands of parishioners and dedicated souls grovel and pray on bended knee, for peace. The multitude have been manipulate through their faith by those that used their power to control through religion. Preaching hell and damnation and that the only way to procure a ticket to heaven was to donate to the Churches coffers each week. Did I not turn the tables of the money lenders in the Synagogue? True wealth, faith and love comes from within the heart.

Do we see happier more joyful souls walking on the Earth? The answer is NO! They remain the oppressed, and the manipulated. They are the ones who sacrifice their lives for those who rage war.

Country against country! Religion against religion! Brother against brother.

When I instructed my disciples to go forward and be *fishers of men* I did not ask them to build churches or create religions. I requested that they go and teach the natural laws of Brotherhood. This was known and written as **The Way**. The Way to find Peace is within the soul, go within."

A small tear slipped down His cheek and He swallowed back the deep emotion of grief, remembering the day of days of condemnation and violence as he kissed his Mother goodbye.

"Please excuse me dear ones. It pains me to witness such turmoil. In my parables the message was simple; to walk with Unconditional Love and Compassion in your hearts, to heal the sick and suffering. To honour their women for each man owes his life to the woman who birthed him. Man and woman were created equal for one cannot do without the other. When Love comes from the heart it is *Divine*. All things can be achieved. I will be with you even to the ends of the Earth.

My Creator / Father gave me the responsibility of governing over the Earth Genesis, whereby I have had occasion to incarnate and to share the wisdom and knowledge of the ages. Now as Earth moves towards *the end times,* as foretold by the Indigenous Ones from long ago, we ask you to carry the message within your soul matrix, *there is no end, no beginning* there is only a recognised time to upgrade the responsibility of *man into* becoming the Divine Human."

Sananda paused to observe the response and smiled. A Light shone from His eyes, encouraging the Peacemakers to see the positive coming event.

"Do you remember another time, another place, when we were gathered on a hillside, on the outskirts of Jerusalem, and I spoke to you in parables of **The Truth and Love**? And on that last day we made an agreement that we would gather again when the time was appropriate. You are now honouring that commitment, for the '*seed*' of the Christ Consciousness is firmly planted within your souls. This is the Light you will carry within. This is the message you will deliver to Gaia and ALL the inhabitants as you move through the coming years of your next incarnation. You are the Brotherhood of Light and Truth, the Light Bearers of the future."

Sananda closed His eyes and a radiant electric blue light shone from His heart charka reaching out to each and everyone present. The Crystal Dome shimmered with His divine energy.

"I will always be with you. Blessings, beloved Peacemakers."

LORD MAITREYA

"Chairman of the Board of Ascended Masters"

"Just as (we) The Galactic Federation have been asked for assistance at this present time, through collective prayer because of turmoil and loss of life - it may also come to pass in your future time - that you too will witness the turmoil and destruction on Planet Earth. Know that in this moment, as you sit before us in service, we give you council to do the same. You, who sit before us, go in *service* for the greater good of ALL. We will honour your collective call, for it shall not reach our station unless it arrives due to critical mass. We HOPE and PRAY this day will never come. WE sincerely trust that your journey will avoid this scenario ever occurring again, for we have complete faith in your motivation for volunteering for these present positions as Light Bearers.

Your success will depend on the weight of darkness that may / or may not descend on humanity during the developing years of commercialism and control. We have seen three potentials in your future. Now it is up to Mankind, how they unfold these probabilities."

Lord MATERIYA stopped in His tracks. There was a blanket of expectation among the audience. The air became still and no one moved.

"Breath! Everyone please take three deep breaths!"

The audience relaxed and the lights went up and flashed a vivid purple tone throughout the Crystal Dome.

"Planet Earth is our most precious and resent genesis. As any proud parent, we have been ever watchful of her progress through the ages. Our last intervention was during the time of the Pyramids when the Sons of the Galactic Federation blended with the children of Earth to secure a new race, to meld an upgrade of DNA. This information has been secreted away from the multitude, although it was clearly written in hieroglyphic text left by your ancestors for all to know. It will be many years before this information is shared with the population but you will be the Ones who forge ahead and reveal the decrypted messages."

Each member present scanned their thought patterns within their soul computer, remembering their journeys in different time frames.

"Now, I have new information for you." Pause. "After much deliberation we have arrived at a collective decision. When you depart on your future life, you will take with you an advanced micro chip of memory which you will access during your years of innocence and which will be updated at astrological time frames. This will allow you to tune into knowledge that will be presented to you to share with your students. It will also give you the communication skills to keep connected to your *spiritual* guides and teachers.

This will assist you when you are being bombarded with negative responses from the set forums of religion, politics and financial institutes. *The Dark Forces of Control.*" Pause.

"Earth's future leaders will come to believe they hold the power and technology to rule through force, manipulation and destruction. If it becomes necessary we will remind them by our very presence 'That It Is Not So'. Intervention is only achievable by Karmic Law, unless the Collective Call goes out for assistance we cannot intervene with Free Will. This is the fail-safe mechanism we have implanted in your consciousness, so that you may call on us when appropriate - so you cannot fail in your mission.

We wish to assure you that each and every one of you, have a precise mission of grand importance within the bigger picture. Every one of you will be connected to Home by a thread of golden light which will act as an invisible matrix, a filament of Divine Love."

Soft music from the Spheres bathed the audience in a golden light announcing the completion of this meeting.

"Please join hands and feel the love flow between you, remember the feeling of connectedness. Breathe in the memory of this day, when we came together as One. Go with our love in your hearts and Our deepest gratitude resting in your soul. Knowing we are ever watchful and supporting your mission."

FINALE

The Ascended Masters gathered in a circle on the dais and joined hands, each Master began to glow a different colour of the rainbow. Their energy started to move in a spiral motion, which ultimately created a circular rainbow. As the vortex speeded up the Masters ascended collectively through the open dome. All those present watched and waited quietly. A few minutes passed before the congregation realized the meeting was complete, they filed out into the sunlight and smiled at each other.

HATHOR and NEXUS

The multitude drifted out of the Crystal Dome filled with inspiration and a little bit of doubt about their future life. The friends gathered under the protective arms of a giant Tulip tree that blushed with an aura of a thousand blooms, and looked at one another expectantly, each one waiting for someone to speak.

"So is everyone still happy with the decision and commitment to return to Earth for this assignment?" Tamara dared to question.

"Yes, yes!" They all replied in one voice.

"We only have a short time to be together, what will we do?" Jacob was eager to hear their thoughts. "I am going to miss you all so much. It has been quite magical being with you all again."

"Well let's do something special." Petra suggested. But they were all saturated with the energy of the gathering and on one could think straight. So they sat comfortably in silence, for a moment that seemed to last an eternity. It was Joel who finally found his voice and broke the silence with a few words of wisdom.

"We have always known about 'The House of many Mansions' so let's go to the Halls of Wisdom, to the Amethyst Palace and refresh our knowledge of crystal energy and how to use it for healing."

"Yes we could also request an audience with Hathor and Nexus our past Mentors. I'm sure they will be waiting for us to arrive."

They quickly picked themselves up, joined hands and headed for the large building which stood in the exquisite grounds on the edge of the Sapphire Lake. From a distance it reminded them of a Scottish Castle.

"Do you remember which entrance to use?" Alistar requested tactfully.

"Yes I do. It's on the North wall we can't see it from here. There is such a magnificent display of Crystals which have been collected from every corner of the Federation. And wait until you see the floor it's made of amethyst and glows with energy like no other. It makes one want to tip-toe across it but that's only an illusion." Esha explained. Her voice notably excited about the coming experience. "I just love coming here. Every time I come Home from an Earth journey I visit Hathor she is just like a Mother figure to me. We share my adventures, cry a little and laugh a lot."

The hefty double oak doors stood open, welcoming many other volunteers as they filed through the grand entrance, all eagerly seeking knowledge and guidance from prestigious Mentors. The group of friends stopped in front of the miniature waterfall and stood still to admire the droplets of water as they kissed clusters of crystals. Many reflected vivid auras with the colours of the rainbow, while others seemed to sing a soft celestial tune.

"Come on we have to climb these stairs to the fourth floor. Isn't the balustrade beautiful? It's all constructed from jade and follows every level to the top floor. Race you!"

As their feet touched the first step the energy was so gentle that they felt as if they were flying on angel wings.

"Wow! That's amazing, does it feel the same when we come down?" asked Joel, he turned back to observe the staircase in wonder.

"Yes it does but your energy will have changed by then so it will feel different again. I never felt the energy the same way twice because each time I have experienced more understandings and that has changed who I am." Esha explained. "This is the door we are wanting. Now everyone stand still, close your eyes." The door seemed to have a personality. Within a few seconds a welcoming face appeared to emerge in the wood panel and smiled a welcome.

"Whom, may I say is calling madam?" The face inquired sincerely.

"It is I. Esha and I have my friends accompanying me. Will you please ask Hathor if we may have an audience with her, please….. Please." Esha giggled and waited patiently.

The face reseeded into the wood panel and the friends all looked at one another in astonishment but remained quiet, waiting in anticipation for the next revelation. The door suddenly opened to reveal a lavish setting. The alabaster walls were draped with silk violet curtains, tied back with beautiful silver tassels. In the centre of the room sat a round ebony coffee table which was carved with beautiful Egyptian hieroglyphic, while large mauve cushions with silver trimmings surround it. The polished mosaic floor reflected their faces like a mirror. Above the door a large symbol of the Sun, and standing on either side of the entrance two gold Lion statues. Outside the full length windows, a circular balcony afforded anyone in the room to soak in the expansive gardens which meandered down to the Blue Lake. Hathor made a grand entrance with arms wide open to receive her guests. Her youthful heart shaped face and large almond eyes had not changed since their last meeting but Esha noticed that her ravishing halo of hair was now streaked with silver threads. Four Siamese cats followed in her wake, her constant companions Ita, Mita, Sita and Pipa.

"Hello! Welcome, this is a wonderful surprise, why are you here?" Without waiting for an answer Hathor scooped Esha up into a warm embrace then turned to greet her friends.

"Hello, I remember each of you from different time frames when we travelled together. I see you are all very excited about your coming journey and that you have many questions. Come on sit down and we will discuss how I may assist you." Hathor herded the group towards the ebony table. "Grab a cushion and make yourselves comfortable."

"This is my partner, Jacob and we have just been to the Rose Bowl to hear the Masters introduce the plans for our next journey. We have all volunteered as peacemakers and we will be leaving very soon. But I just had to come and see you before we go to the birthing chamber. We all did." Esha gabbled on while her friends sat patiently waiting to have their questions answered.

"Slow down dear child, we still have plenty of time." Hathor gently reminded her. "Oh these are exciting times."

Ruth quickly seized the moment, "You should have seen the butterflies. They delivered our sustenance on their wings. They were so beautiful; they all arrived at the same time through the opening in the roof. And the food was so delicious I don't think I have experienced those flavours before."

Hathor acknowledged the magnificent display. "Those of us who were absent connected through a visual link and I did see the butterflies. What a truly amazing sight. And I saw your faces in the crowd. You all looked radiant as you listened intently to the information being offered. In that moment I was so proud of you all for your courage and dedication."

"Hathor, do you really believe we are prepared for this journey? We did get swept up in the energy of the collective consciousness while we were all gathered together with one vision but there is still a bit of reservation as to wether we are well gifted with the necessary talents to give of our best." Alistar questioned sincerely, the group needed sound conformation.

"Oh yes, I am quite confident you are all well imbued with sufficient knowledge and understanding of the human condition to be able complete your contracts. And while we are gathered here I am going to impart a small seminar on crystal magic and colour therapy." Her smile spread from ear to ear and lighted up her eyes with excitement. Hathor turned to her four companions, "Dear Ones, will you please sit on the four corners of the compass as practiced in times gone and then we will begin." Ita, Mita, Sita and Pipa sauntered to their respective posts around the ebony coffee table, sat to attention and purred with contentment.

Immediately a holographic vision appeared in the middle of the table and the crystals presented themselves one by one.

"WE are from the Mineral Kingdom and guardians of the Balance of Gaia and that is why we are seldom seen on the surface of the Earth. Our world is deep within where we are left to our own purpose. Many civilisations through the Ages have sort our magnificence for adornment, but we also offer the cosmic energy for healing. Our colours resonate to the human aura and chakra centres which govern specific organs of the human biology. Our colours also align to the Rainbow which is a reflection of the Spiritual nature of Man." There was a pause to allow those present to absorb the concept. "Man still does not recognise the full concept that they are an integral part of the Whole. Every aspect, of their world is inter-related through the gifts of Nature, such as the Plant Kingdom, the Animal Kingdom and our own Mineral Kingdom. We are all One. If there were one part absent there would be no balance. When the Masters created the new Genesis it took many millennium of fine tuning to discover the correct ratios to define and bring about perfect balance." Another, long pause.

"Why are WE explaining all this, at this present time? Because when you arrive in your projected time frame you will witness the abusive nature of Man as he rapes and pledgees the Earth of her buried treasures for industrial greed and power. Your world will be exploited beyond reason. Why am I sharing this information? Because I come with a plea, that during your mission you vow to protect our Kingdom. Dear peacemakers, we give you authority to assess our cosmic healing energies, as we have presented our qualities to you this day but we now humbly ask for prudence in the commercial world of trade. Can you assist us?" The collective voice softly requested.

Hathor quietly observed their reaction while the gang listened intently to every word. "This is one of the reasons you felt the urge to visit me before you journey forward. The Crystals spoke with me soon after the Masters imparted their guidance, and requested this forum. Now you can understand there is a bigger picture. This whole scenario will also be linked to environmental damage if there is not a tight control on conditions."

The gang sat there with confusion marked on their faces, each desperately trying to envisage the future potentials.

"We now present the Crystal Charts for Healing Service which will also be updated as we deemed appropriate, in agreement with the Crystal Kingdom."

CRYSTAL AWARENESS GUIDE
by LEGION OF LIGHT
THE TRANSFORMATIONAL PROPERTIES OF GEMS AND MINERALS

AGATE — A variety of chalcedony. Tones and strengthens body/mind. Imparts a sense of strength and courage. Facilitates ability to discern truth and accept circumstances. Grounding, but energetic. Powerful healer. Works with chakras and attitudes according to color of stone.

ALEXANDRITE — A variety of chrysoberyl. Aids internal and external regeneration. Has positive influence on nervous system, spleen, pancreas. Helps to align mental and emotional body. Spiritual transformation and regeneration. Reflects highest potentials or unfoldment. Joy, oneness with life. Chakra(s): crown.

AMAZONITE — A variety of feldspar. Soothes nervous system. Strengthens heart and physical body. Aids alignment of mental and etheric body. Brings joy and upliftment. Creative expression. Facilitates clearer vision of one's own harmful tendencies, making them easier to release. Chakra(s): throat.

AMBER — Fossilized resin from prehistoric pine trees. Exerts positive influence on endocrine system, spleen, heart. Healing, soothing, harmonizing. Electrically alive with solidified golden light. Stabilizes kundalini awakening. Activates altruistic nature. Spiritualizes the intellect. Chakra(s): navel, solar plexus, crown.

AMETHYST — A variety of quartz. Strengthens endocrine and immune systems. Enhances right brain activity and pineal and pituitary glands. Powerful blood cleanser and energizer. Helps mental disorders. Purification and regeneration on all levels of consciousness. Transmutes one's lower nature into the more highly refined aspects of their higher potentials. Physical representative of the Violet Ray of alchemy and transformation. Cuts through illusion. Enhances psychic abilities. Excellent for meditation. Aids channeling abilities. Calming, strong protective qualities. Healing, divine love, inspiration, intuition. Chakra(s): third eye, crown.

AQUAMARINE — A variety of beryl. Calms nerves, reduces fluid retention. Strengthens kidneys, liver, spleen, thyroid. Purifies the body. Enhances clarity of mind, aids creative self-expression. Physical/emotional/mental balancer. Helps banish fears and phobias. Excellent for meditation, inspiration, peace, calmness, love. Chakra(s): throat, solar plexus.

AVENTURINE (Green) — A variety of quartz. Purifies mental, emotional and etheric bodies. Aids in releasing anxiety and fear. Stimulates muscle tissue. Strengthens blood. Emotional tranquility, positive attitudes towards life. Brings one into alignment with their cosmic independence. Health, wellbeing. Chakra(s): heart.

AZURITE — Enhances flow of energy through nervous system (because of copper content). Helps body utilize oxygen. Strengthens blood. Facilitates clear meditation. Cuts through illusion. Enhances psychic abilities. Initiates transformation. Cleanses mental body. Inspiration, creativity, intuition. Chakra(s): third eye, throat.

BLOODSTONE — A variety of chalcedony. Strengthens and oxygenates bloodstream. Enhances physical/mental vitality. Strengthens heart, spleen, bone marrow. Aids in balancing iron deficiencies. Reduces emotional/mental stress. Powerful physical healer. Stimulates movement of kundalini. Links root chakra with heart. Inner guidance, altruism, idealism. A highly evolved mineral. Chakra(s): root, heart.

CALCITE — Aids kidneys, pancreas, spleen. Balances male/female polarities. Alleviates fear, reduces stress. Emotionally balancing. Grounds excess energy. Increases capacity for astral projection. Joy, lightness. Works with chakras and attitudes by color of stone.

CARNELIAN — A variety of chalcedony. Very highly evolved mineral healer. Energizes blood. Aids kidneys, lungs, liver, gallbladder, pancreas. Aids tissue regeneration. Vitalizes physical/emotional/mental bodies. Aligns physical and etheric bodies. Enhances attunement with inner self. Facilitates concentration. Opens the heart. Warming, social, joyous. Chakra(s): navel, solar plexus, heart.

CELESTITE — Enhances thyroid functions. Reduces stress. Relaxing, peace of mind. Accelerates growth. Aids personal creative expression. Helps one adjust to higher, more rarefied states of awareness. Truth, reliability. Clear speech. Chakra(s): throat.

CHRYSOCOLLA — Aids in preventing ulcers, digestive problems, arthritic conditions. Strengthens lungs and thyroid gland. Enhances metabolism. Excellent for female disorders. Alleviates fears, guilt, tension. Helps clear subconscious imbalances. Activates feminine qualities. Amplifies throat chakra — creative expression, power, communication. Joy, emotional balance. Chakra(s): heart, throat.

CHRYSOPRASE — A variety of quartz. Balances neurotic patterns. Eases depression and sexual imbalances. Fertility. Calming, balancing, healing for physical/emotional/mental bodies. Helps one see clearly into personal problems. Brings out inner talents. Lightheartedness, joy. Chakra(s): heart.

CITRINE — A variety of quartz. Good for kidneys, colon, liver, gallbladder, digestive organs, heart. Tissue regeneration. Detoxifies physical/emotional/mental bodies. Enhances body's healing energy. Diminishes self-destructive tendencies. Raises self-esteem. Powerful alignment with Higher Self. Lightheartedness, cheerfulness, hope. Warming, energizing. Attracts abundance. Chakra(s): navel, crown.

COPPER — Influences flow of blood. Supplies strong energy to body/mind. Aids metabolism. Helps detoxify body. An aid for exhaustion and sexual imbalance. Aligns physical/emotional bodies. Raises self-esteem. Strong conductor of energy.

DIAMOND — Enhances brain functions. Aids alignment of cranial bones. Breaks up blockages in crown chakra and in the personality. Master healer. Dispels negativity. Purifies physical/etheric bodies. Reflects will and power aspects of God. Enhances full spectrum of energies in body/mind/spirit. Alignment with Higher Self. Abundance, innocence, purity, faithfulness. Chakra(s): all.

DIOPTASE — Strengthens cardiovascular and central nervous systems. Excellent aid for ulcers, nervous stomach, heart troubles, blood pressure. Vitalizes, balances, tones body/mind. Emotional stability. Peace of mind. Excellent for use with healing and affirmations. Abundance, prosperity, progress, health, well being. Chakra(s): heart.

EMERALD — A variety of beryl. Strengthens heart, liver, kidneys, immune system, nervous system. Tonic for body/mind/spirit. Aids alignment in subtle bodies. Enhances dreams, meditation, deeper spiritual insight. Represents the potential of divinity within us. Prosperity, love, kindness, tranquility, balance, healing, patience. Strong emotional balancer. Chakra(s): heart, solar plexus.

FLUORITE — Strengthens teeth and bones. Improves absorption of vital nutrients. Beneficial for blood vessels and spleen. Grounds excess energy. Excellent for advancement of mind, greater concentration, meditation. Helps one grasp higher, more abstract concepts. Facilitates interdimensional communication. Powerful healer. Works with chakras and attitudes according to color of stone.

GARNET (Red) — Strengthens, purifies, vitalizes and regenerates bodily systems, especially the bloodstream. Has strong affinity with root chakra, helping to harmonize the potent forces of the kundalini. Stimulates pituitary gland. Aligns subtle bodies. Love, compassion. Enhances imagination. Chakra(s): root, heart.

GOLD — Purifies and energizes physical body. Improves circulation, strengthens nervous system. Balances and develops heart chakra. Balances hemisphere of brain. Aids tissue regeneration. Attracts positive energy into aura. Amplifies thought forms, Aids personal illumination. Solar energy, male aspect. Chakra(s): navel, heart and crown.

HEMATITE — Has positive effect upon bloodstream. Activates spleen. Increases resistance to stress. Helps circulate oxygen throughout body. Strengthens physical and etheric bodies. Energizing, vitalizing. Enhances personal magnetism, optimism, will, courage. Slightly grounding. Powerful stone for those attracted to it.

HERKIMER DIAMOND — A type of quartz crystal. Cleanses subtle bodies. Reduces stress. Balances and purifies energy within body/mind. Similar qualities as clear quartz. Powerful amplifier. Enhances inner vision. Increases awareness of dreams — "dream crystal". Stores thought forms and information. Chakra(s): all.

JADE — Strengthens heart, kidneys, immune system. Helps cleanse blood. Increases longevity and fertility. Aids eye disorders and female problems. Powerful emotional balancer. Radiates divine, unconditional love. Clarity, modesty, courage, justice, wisdom. Peaceful and nurturing. Dispels negativity. Healing affinity will correspond to particular color of stone.

JASPER (All Colors) — A variety of chalcedony. Strengthens liver, gallbladder, bladder. Powerful healer, main aspect on physical body. Represents earth element. Works with chakras and attitudes according to color of stone.

KUNZITE (Pink Spodumene) — High lithium content makes Kunzite beneficial to individuals with addictive behavior. Strengthens cardiovascular system. Aids manic depression. Excellent balance for physical/emotional/mental bodies. Powerful stone for opening/healing heart. Helps one surrender to Higher Self. Enhances self-esteem. Tolerance, acceptance. Soothing, calming. Chakra(s): heart.

KYANITE — Strengthens throat chakra. Enhances creative expression, communication, truth, loyalty, reliability, serenity. Connection to causal plane. Facilitates astral/interdimensional travel. Chakra(s): throat, third eye.

LAPIS LAZULI — Strengthens skeletal system. Activates thyroid gland. Releases tension and anxiety. Energizes throat chakra. Augments strength, vitality, virility. Facilitates opening of chakras. Mental clarity, illumination. Enhances psychic abilities and communication with Higher Self and Spirit Guides. Creative expression. Chakra(s): third eye, throat.

LEPIDOLITE — Aids muscles, strengthens heart, beneficially oxygenates blood. High lithium content aids emotional/mental balance and stability. Aids sleep. Enhances expression of one's inner light and joy. Chakra(s): heart.

MALACHITE — Aids functions of pancreas and spleen. Reduces stress and tension. Aids tissue regeneration. Strengthens heart, circulatory system, pineal and pituitary glands. Aids sleep. Vitalizing for body/mind. Reveals subconscious blocks. Excellent balancer on all levels. Chakra(s): heart, solar plexus.

CRYSTAL AWARENESS GUIDE
by LEGION OF LIGHT
THE TRANSFORMATIONAL PROPERTIES OF GEMS AND MINERALS

MOLDAVITE — A deep green, silica based tektite (meteorite) that fell to Earth about 15 million years ago. Aids alignment with Higher Self. Balancing and healing for physical body/mind. Aids in channeling extraterrestrial and inter-dimensional sources. Chakra(s): heart, third eye.

METEORITE — Helps reveal past lives from other planets and galaxies. Enhances connection with extraterrestrial energies. Expands awareness. Similar to obsidian, but denser. Chakra(s): root.

MOONSTONE — Has healing affinity with stomach, spleen, pancreas, pituitary gland. Unblocks lymphatic system. Relieves anxiety and stress. Aids birthing process, helps female problems. Emotional balancer, helps lessen tendency to over-react emotionally. Flexibility in attitudes. Aligns emotions with Higher Self. Chakra(s): heart.

OBSIDIAN — Beneficially influences stomach and intestines. Connects mind and emotions. Slightly masculine energy. Grounds spiritual energy into physical plane. Absorbs and dispenses negativity. Reduces stress. Helps clear subconscious blocks. Brings an understanding of silence and "the void." Detachment, but with wisdom and love. Powerful healer for those returned with it. Chakra(s): root.

ONYX — A variety of chalcedony. Relieves stress. Balances male/female polarities. Strengthens bone marrow. Aids detachment. Enhances emotional balance and self-control. Higher inspiration. Works with chakras and attributes according to color of stone.

OPAL — Stimulates pineal and pituitary glands. Aids eyesight. Emotional balancer. Enhances intuition. The full spectrum of colors resonates with all chakras. Helps conscious connection with highest aspects of being. Chakra(s): heart and others, depending on color.

PERIDOT (Olivine) — Balances glandular system. Aids tissue regeneration. Has beneficial influence on heart, pancreas, spleen, liver, adrenals. Purifies body. Enhances bloodstream. Overall balancer and tonic for body/mind. Aligns subtle bodies. Increases intuitive awareness. Reduces stress. Stimulates mind. Accelerates personal growth, opens new doors of opportunity. Chakra(s): navel, solar plexus, heart.

PYRITE — Aids digestion, improves circulation. Strengthens and oxygenates blood. Enhances brain functions. Influences a more positive outlook on life. Enhances emotional body, strengthens will. Helps one's ability to work with others harmoniously. Practicality. Chakra(s): root, solar plexus, heart.

QUARTZ CRYSTAL (Clear) — Enhances the crystalline properties of blood, body and mind. Activates and enhances pineal and pituitary glands. Emotional balancer. Stimulates brain functions. Amplifies thought forms. Full spectrum energy activates all levels of consciousness. Dispels negativity in one's energy field and in environment. Receives, activates, stores, transmits and amplifies energy. Excellent for meditation. Enhances interdimensional communication and communication with Higher Self and Spirit Guides. Chakra(s): all.

RHODOCHROSITE — Aids spleen, kidneys, heart, pituitary gland and circulation of blood. Enhances memory and intellectual power. Emotional balancer. Helps heal emotional wounds and traumas. Aligns subtle bodies. Red/pink color helps to blend courage/well/compassion aspects of lower chakras with loving expression of the heart. Divine love, acceptance of self and life. Powerful healer for those attuned to this stone. Chakra(s): root, heart.

RHODONITE — Aids central nervous system, thyroid gland, body reflexes, pituitary gland, pancreas. Strengthens immunity. Improves memory. Eases physical/emotional trauma. Reduces stress, calms mind. Aligns root and heart chakras for bringing love into action and manifestation (red and black variety). Self-esteem, confidence. Enhances energy levels of body/mind. Pink variety (without blacks) helps impart understanding of strength within softer ability. Great stone for light-workers serving in crisis. Chakra(s): root, heart.

ROSE QUARTZ — Aids kidneys and circulatory system. Increases fertility. Eases sexual/emotional imbalances. Helps clear stored anger, resentment, guilt, fear, jealousy. Reduces stress and tension, cools hot temper. Enhances self-confidence and creativity. Aids development of forgiveness, compassion, love. "Love stone." Chakra(s): heart.

RUBY — Aids regeneration of physical/spiritual heart. Enhances circulation. Vitalizes blood and entire body/mind system. Strengthens immunity. Activates sluggish or dormant conditions on physical/spiritual levels. Refines lower passions. Courage, integrity, selfless service, joy, spiritual devotion, power, leadership. Helps banish sense of limitation. Chakra(s): root, heart.

RUTILATED QUARTZ — Regeneration of tissue throughout body. Enhances life-force. Strengthens immune system. Stimulates brain functions. Eases depression, facilitates inspiration, increases clairvoyance. Highly electrical, more intensity than clear quartz. Pierces through layers of physical/emotional/mental density. Transmutes negativity. Enhances communication with Higher Self and Spirit Guides. Very powerful healer. Chakra(s): all.

SMOKY QUARTZ — Strengthens adrenals, kidneys, pancreas. Increases fertility, balances sexual energy. Aids depression. Mildly sedative and relaxing. Initiates movement of kundalini. Dissipates subconscious blocks and negativity on all levels. Grounding, centering. Excellent for meditation. Enhances dream awareness and channeling abilities. Chakra(s): root, navel, solar plexus.

SUGILITE (Royal Azel) — Enhances functions of pineal, pituitary and adrenal glands. Activates and balances brain hemispheres. Strengthens heart. Aids physical healing and purification of bodily systems. Emotional balancer, reduces stress. Brings higher spiritual awareness into physical reality. Enhances sensitivity. Strong protective qualities. Excellent for meditation. Enhances channeling abilities. Chakra(s): third eye, crown.

SODALITE — Aids pancreas, balances endocrine system, strengthens metabolism and lymphatic system. Balances male/female polarities. Alleviates fear. Calms and clears the mind. Slightly sedative, grounding. Cuts through density and illusion, bringing clarity and truth. Enhances communication, creative expression. Similar qualities as lapis lazuli. Chakra(s): throat, third eye.

SAPPHIRE — Strengthens heart and kidneys. Activates pituitary gland thereby aiding entire glandular system. Aligns body/mind/spirit. Stimulates psychic abilities, clarity and inspiration. Creative expression, loyalty, love. Aids connection with Higher Self/Spirit Guides. Strengthens will. Expands cosmic awareness. Dispels confusion. Excellent for meditation. Chakra(s): throat, third eye.

SELENITE (Gypsum) — Strengthens bones, teeth. Soothes nerves. Has positive effect on brain, aiding power of concentration and clarity. Enhances willpower. Grounded white light. Chakra(s): crown.

SILVER — Enhances mental functions. Aids circulation. Strengthens blood, physically and etherically. Strengthens pineal and pituitary glands. Relieves stress. Relates to the moon, subconscious, female aspect. Emotional balance. Speech improvement. Excellent energy conductor.

TIGER EYE — Variety of chalcedony (quartz). Beneficial for spleen, pancreas, digestive organs, colon. Emotional balancer. Enhances connection with personal power and will. Grounding, centering. Helps soften stubbornness. Enhances clear perception and insight. Slightly masculine energy. Chakra(s): navel, solar plexus.

TOPAZ — (Gold Topaz) — Tissue regeneration. Strengthens liver, gallbladder, spleen, digestive organs, nervous system. Detoxifies body. Warming, awakening, inspiring. Absorbance. Chakra(s): navel, crown. (Blue Topaz) — Tissue regeneration. Strengthens thyroid gland, enhances metabolism. Emotional balance. Cooling, soothing, peace, tranquility. Creativity, self-expression. Enhances psychic perception, communication with Higher Self/Spirit Guides. Chakra(s): heart, throat, third eye.

TOURMALINE (All Colors) — Aids balance of endocrine system. Aids sleep. Strengthens, vitalizes body/mind. Activates and enhances crystalline properties of body/mind. Aligns subtle bodies. Dispels fear and negative conditions. Strong protective influence. Concentration, inspiration. Enhances sensitivity and understanding. Powerful healer, highly electrical. The various colors will activate and align corresponding chakras: Black Tourmaline (Schorl) — root. Watermelon Tourmaline (red/green) — root, heart. Green Tourmaline — heart. Blue Tourmaline (Indicolite) — throat, third eye. Red/Pink Tourmaline (Rubellite) — root, heart.

TOURMALINATED QUARTZ — Clear quartz with black tourmaline crystals inside. Balances male/female polarities. Aids in balancing extremes. Grounding, very protective, dissipates negativity. Combines forces of clear quartz and black tourmaline. Chakra(s): root, crown.

TURQUOISE — Toner, strengthens entire body. Tissue regeneration. Aids circulation, lungs, respiratory system. Vitalizes blood, nervous system. Aligns chakras. Enhances meditation. Creative expression, peace of mind, emotional balance, communication, friendship, loyalty. Chakra(s): throat.

VARISCITE — Soothing, calming, balancing for body/mind. Aids blood, heart. Emotional stability. Helps one recall past lives. Self confidence. Abundance. Chakra(s): heart, solar plexus.

ZIRCON (Hyacinth) — Strengthens the mind. Aids bowel problems. Balances pituitary and pineal glands. Aligns subtle bodies. Emotional balance, self esteem. Aids sleep. Similar properties as diamond and quartz crystal. All around healer. Chakra(s): all.

NOTE: Crystals, gems and other minerals are wonderful tools for transformations. They are "solid friends" and objects of beauty that can help us along the way to our goal. We must remember, however, that crystals, gems and minerals are a solidified reflection of that which is always available within ourselves, and that love is the only goal. Let's keep everything in proper perspective, not giving our power away, while enjoying all the gifts that nature has provided for us. Love is all that matters. Love one another!

"When gems are gathered for adornment there is little disturbance in the Earth energy but when the Mineral kingdom is distributed from one country to another, this changes the energy field and balance. The Earths axis was carefully set to create harmony." Hathor informed them.

"Yes I see what you are saying. The original engineers calculated for a stable environment that would not be manipulated through man and yet flexible to create its own changes when necessary to project harmony." Joel offered his knowledge and wisdom.

"The word *progress* is often bantered around by the commercial world but one truly has to be prudent as to what that really means. Progress is not always in the best interest of the Planet and can quickly disrupt the ecology beyond repair." Hathor paused trying to decide wether to recall past mistakes from long ago. "When we first came to the new Genesis we built magnificent cities and were highly skilled. Our leaders were brilliant far seeing visionaries and all the kingdoms lived in harmony for thousands of years until the energy of duality changed our perception of who we were. Gradually the negative forces grew stronger and flexed their muscles, with the visitation of the Dark Overloads came the energy of greed. Eventually we managed to destroy our world through the misuse of Crystal power and you all know the consequences of that scenario. The Creator had no choice but to send the deluge to cleanse the Earth of the negative ions. The word *progress* is only related to bringing about and producing harmony."

"So what the crystals are saying is remember what happened in the distant past." Joel queried, still trying to get a handle on the deep message being transmitted.

"We always say there is a time and place for everything and that everything is happening at the right time. But this time frame is reaching a very insecure passage and we are imparting knowledge for you to assess when the time is right." Hathor replied in a serious tone. "Your challenges will be great."

"The picture is getting clearer but much more complicated. There seems to be a huge amount of issues to contend with during this future life." Ruth's face looked down hearted as she turned to the gang. "Do you reckon we are up to this?"

"Well I must admit it seems to be getting more complicated by the minute." Isobel replied looking around at her friends for support.

Tyler seized the moment to intervene, "Don't get down hearted too soon.

Let's recognise that we have been given this new information to take with us, we are already out in front and have a greater understanding of the part that the crystals are going to play."

"Thank you Tyler, you are quite right. Knowledge is power to make decisions and change the world and isn't that what your future is all about? Isn't it going to be exciting? I shall watch your progress with great enthusiasm and also be there to guide you. I think my work will be cut out for me." Hathor smiled with reassurance.

"You're right, we can do this." Esha affirmed giving Jacobs arm a squeeze and looking at her friends for conformation.

"Okay, okay yes we can do all of this and more or we wouldn't be sitting here now." Jacob picked up the thread of confidence and passed it around the room.

Hathor quickly intervened while their spirits were rising, "Shall we have some refreshments now before you leave to have your audience with Nexus. I know he is expecting you to arrive within the hour." While they were on a high note she decided that they had received sufficient information. She clicked her fingers and the hologram disappeared.

While the early morning dew still blessed the emerald lawn, Hathor had walked down to visit the Sapphire Lake and collected a basket of white lotus petals. When she returned to her kitchen, Hathor set about grinding them with fresh honey and then added the mixture to a mulled wine to create a delicious drink. Now she poured the amber liquid into copper goblets to serve to her young guests. This ancient recipe is renowned to lift the spirits. Hathor glided into the room carrying a large silver tray and placed it on the ebony coffee table, "Try this new beverage I put together this morning, I think you will find it quite divine. And then it will be time for our farewells. My blessings go with you and I will watch over you until we meet again."

"Umm, this is brilliant, can't say I've tasted anything like it before." They all agreed and quickly emptied their goblets.

Hathor escorted them to the door and gave them each a Motherly hug, "Nexus is on the top floor. I am sure he has some very intriguing information for you, so listen carefully. Off you go now."

* * * * *

The door stood wide open to welcome them and they could hear Nexus humming a soft melody while engrossed with a new invention. There were no visible signs but they could feel his essence and enthusiasm seeping out of every corner. The room was lined with huge book-shelves that touch the ceiling. As they entered it felt like walking into Aladdin's Cave. A massive wooden carved table filled the centre of the room. And a large skylight permeated the room, illuminating ancient scrolls that were scattered on every chair and available resting place.

"Hello. Where are you?" Liam called out announcing their arrival.

Nexus appeared from behind a screen his hoary face painted with a wide smile of welcome.

"Come in, come in." He waved as he rolled down the sleeves of his ornate cloak and stroked his wiry, white beard into form, and then he quickly straightened his velvet cap which appeared to have slipped over one eye and pulled the gold girdle tight around his waist.

"Ah there you are my young friends I have been expecting you. Come on in, we will move some of this mess and find a place where we can communicate." He beckoned them to enter and quickly rearranged the manuscripts to yet another resting place.

"You always seem to be so busy I hope we are not taking up your time?" Ruth questioned as she walked into the room observing the layers of dust that clung to the shelves.

"You all look wonderful, so young and full of energy and expectation. I hear you are about to embark on a very exciting journey. My days of adventures are over, as you know my last visit to Earth was many years ago and my mission fraught with secrecy. We are not always appreciated for the messages we bring to mankind. My name was Nostradamus and I documented the passageway of the times to come, as guidance for future events. But never mind all that, it is well in the past, we must concentrate on your new time frame. Come on take a seat and we will get busy with coming events." Nexus quickly shuffled books, papers and old manuscripts to clear a space. "Please be seated."

The gang were silent as they observed the Master and waited patiently to ask their questions. The mulled wine had softened their energy and relaxed their thought patterns.

"Now where will we begin?" Nexus spoke out loud but he was really talking to himself. He put his head in his hands as if trying to detach from his previous project, mentally preparing his thoughts in a special sequence before delivering his wisdom to the expectant group.

The gang waited for a moment and they suspected that Nexus had nodded off into a deep sleep. They looked at each other and smiled, waited. Then quite suddenly Nexus startled them with his voice.

"I have looked through the window of *time* to see your challenges. Our recommendation is that you protect Mother Earth at all costs from pollution and toxic waste. During the past 20years we have seen the beginning of the Industrial era with many great inventions improving the quality of life and transportation, with progress there comes the responsibility of due care for the planet. During your lifetime this problem of waste products will become crucial on many levels. While we sit here you cannot possibly image what I am trying to convey to you. So I employ you to remember my words." Pause.

"I foresee a time when the oceans will be so contaminated with toxic waste, that this condition will choke the waterways and all living things therein. The food chain will be depleted of basic food supplies for a stable diet. You must protect the great creatures of the deep for they will head towards extinction and upset the balance of wisdom." He reached out to touch Alistar's hand, "You will be in the land that starts the reform to protect these creatures and bring this ecological disaster to the world's attention."

"I see but how will I achieve this? At this moment what you speak of seems outrageous and would appear insurmountable."

"You are returning to Earth as a peacemaker, there will be many who will join your leadership and use peaceful means, offer funds and become a collective voice." Nexus replied in a serious tone. "It will come about."

"Will we be part of this organisation? We will be in Australia." Isobel and Tyler requested. "We are all supposed to meet up as a group."

"You will assist in a different way, through paper scrolls. There will be much to see too." Nexus stood up and started to pace the floor, his hands locked behind his back, his eyes focused on the floor. No one moved while the Master contemplated his thoughts. Time stood still for ten minutes and then he returned to his chair satisfied with the knowledge he was about to impart.

"The Pen is mightier than the Sword, my friends. Why do I say this? Because my written words from long ago still live on and will be studied for reference in the times to come and you will be part of the resurrection of my prophesies. The program for this Genesis was set out in a progressive matrix, within a set time scale but when *free will* is ordained there are many directions it can take. We see great potentials but unfortunately there are also many choices, which can be confusing and not always constructive. The children of Earth must reach maturity and come to understand there purpose and that is, to become Enlightened Beings. Take your knowledge and write the words from your heart. Write them in parables or fairy tales, fact or fiction and share your personal experiences with truth and compassion."

"That sounds very exciting but do you think we will have enough time to fit all this extra work into our busy agenda?"

Isobel already felt saturated with information about their coming journey.

"Some of this writing will be connected to your vocation and will be accomplished in your middle years. So do not worry now. Alistar and Joel will be interested in bringing groups together for extended personal studies and can assess journals to write articles. Jacob and Liam will find their interests shift towards science and new inventions that will conserve energy on the planet." Nexus explained in a calm voice.

"Well that sounds exciting and very stimulating too me. Tell us some more." Liam requested eager to get a greater understanding of his future work.

"Tyler you can prepare young minds to care for the planet, to grow fresh fruit and vegetables and use the old ways of preparing the land because in time they will forget. Those that work with the land will supply the multitude that live in the city and will not necessarily be appreciated for their dedication of replenishing the food chain." Nexus turned to the girls and studied their faces for a moment.

"And you will teach the female population to stand up and find their worth, for men and women were put on the Earth as equals, a perfect balance to compliment each other. Human kind cannot live in harmony until this is recognised in the mind and soul."

Nexus moved towards the large window and looked out upon the land and observed the brilliant colours of the azalea bushes and the large rosettes of the magnolia flowers. All lay in perfect harmony. Without turning, he clicked his fingers and a parchment scroll appeared in front of each student.

"I have investigated your astrology charts and they are there to inform you of the self knowledge you will require. Please read them carefully." Nexus remained stationery and waited patiently. All was quiet for 30 minutes. He then walked back to join his students. "Well I hope this has added a new dimension to knowing your future persona and empowered you with inner knowledge."

"Thank you, Nexus." A chorus of voices replied.

"I now recommend that you all take a short break and enjoy a walk in the garden to refresh yourselves, breath some energy. I will see you back here in 1 hour and we will continue with further instructions."

* * * * *

The friends marched in single file out the door and headed towards the flight of stairs, "I wonder if we get the same feeling of floating going down as we did coming up," Tamara giggled wanting to be the first one to find out. "Come on."

"It's like being in an energy field," Joel remarked but his attention was more on how it worked.

"Oh I like this much better than those bumpy lifts we get on Earth, they are scary and when you step inside the floor seems to drop a couple of inches before you feel your feet on steady ground." Petra spoke her thoughts out loud. She held out her arms and it felt like flying without the wind.

They quickly arrived back at the huge, double Oak doors and tumbled out into the sunshine. To the far right of the building they found a large stand of Eucalyptus trees, "Have any of you seen those species of trees before? They don't look familiar to me, let's go and see what they are about." Alistar suggested, for some unknown reason he felt drawn to the setting, almost as if it were pulling him to enter.

"Well I don't think they are native trees to this land. Did anyone see them when we arrived here," Ruth queried.

"No!" They replied collectively. "Are they real or is this whole picture a hologram?"

"It must be there for a reason. Maybe its here for us to explore and maybe it holds some exciting information for us to find." Esha suggested as her imagination started to run riot, "I wonder what we will find?" She ducked her head and crept forward between the arch of tall gum trees and the others followed her with expectation.

"Maybe there's someone here to give us a guided tour." Alistar suggested.

"Or maybe, we just have to discover what's here for us and try to put the picture together." Ruth butted in with her logical mind. "There must be a good reason for this adventure."

They continued through the undergrowth, "Do you feel as if someone is watching us?" Tyler scanned the tree tops expecting to see a pair of eyes following them but for the moment could not trace the feeling.

"What are you looking for?" Isobel queried and while she was looking up almost tripped over a log on the pathway.

"The bees are enjoying the nectar from these blossoms and if you look hard enough there seems to be nuts on the branches too. I suppose the nuts carry the seeds. Most, unusual!" Jacob had been studying the clusters of bright red frilly flowers. "Tyler, I have found those pair of eyes you were feeling. Look everyone there's a grey kind of small bear sitting between the fork in the branches of that tree and it's feeding on the leaves."

Everyone rushed to the base of the tree and craned their necks upwards to catch a glimpse of the creature. "Have any of you seen this creature before?" Esha questioned her friends.

As they stood and watched in fascination, the bear informed them in a quiet melodic voice, "I am a Koala bear and I am a native of the land called Australia. These eucalypts are my stable diet and I am a protected species. You have been offered an advanced journey of this ancient land, the land you will be settling on, during your next lifetime. My friends and I are here to give you a quick tour. We come to ask that you protect our environment and food chain because man will encroach upon our habitat, for urbanisation and industrial ventures and our homes will be rapidly destroyed."

"Wow! Did you hear that, a bear that talks?" Tamara stood and watched the creature in wonder. "Isn't he the sweetest thing?"

"Where are we?" Liam asked politely, he turned back to investigate where they had entered but could see no visible signs. "The doorway has vanished, so which way do we go?"

"What do you mean the doorway has closed?" Joel searched for an opening. "You are right it's not there. There must be some kind of directions somewhere. Come on help me look for a signal."

"Do not concern yourself young master. This short journey has been arranged to give you insight of a land you have never visited before. An ancient land that remained pristine for this future time. Here we will reveal to you some of its wonders. We are also part of the future plan." Spoke the Koala, clearly unperturbed with their presence.

"I see." Jacob replied, studying the Koala. "Can you please move a little closer so we may meet you, in person? My name is Jacob and these are my friends." The Koala moved to a lower branch and inspected them for their sincerity. Jacob noted the soft grey fur and large round fluffy ears, the small black eyes and sharp long claws, and that Koala was not a large bear.

"We will meet again when you settle in Margaret River and you walk among the Tall trees. For now you must keep moving, there are other creatures waiting. You will find directions as you move forward that will guide your pathway. No harm will come to you while you remain within this energy field. It was a pleasure to meet you all and now you must be on your way. Farewell." Koala quickly climbed to a higher branch where his mate and offspring were waiting.

While everyone was concerned about the directions Esha had spotted a rare species of fauna growing on the forest floor, "Come and look at this amazing spider orchid, it's so dainty and just look at the depth of colour. Have you seen this species before? It's so small, one could easily have missed it."

"Come on Esha we don't have all day." Alistar wanted to move on and kept a lookout for the directions. "Oh here it is. An arrow has appeared on the trunk of this large Ghost gum, so we must have to walk this way."

"Where is the path taking us too?" There came a squawking sound and a flutter of white wings, a large yellow crested Cockatoo dropped in front of their pathway and the friends quickly came to a sudden halt.

"Hello! Hello! Where are you going?" The Cockatoo inquired bobbing up and down as if he were dancing. "Are you looking for me?"

"We don't know, we were guided to walk through this forest when we met Koala and now we are following the signals." Petra replied in a soft voice not wanting to alarm the bird. "Where we meant to meet you?"

"Yes, there are many animals and creatures waiting to greet you. They asked me to inspect how far you had journeyed and that is why I am here.

Come on hurry along." The cockatoo waddled along the path, chirping away to himself. Within an instant, the remainder of the flock descended from the tree tops like a cloud of snowflakes, to join him and gathered around their feet. "Walk this way please, follow us."

Suddenly the pathway opened onto a vast plain of red dust and spinefax bushes with a cloudless blue sky. In the middle of the picture there was a small billabong surrounded by many native creatures that are required to travel great distances to reach a watering hole.

"My job is done now have fun." With that the flock took flight and returned to the forest tree tops.

The gang moved forward until they stood on the edge of the water-hole.

Ruth stood very still as a large bird with very a long neck and very powerful legs approached her, "Hello, I am Emu." Emu fluttered her eyelashes and lowered her head to make eye contact. "Do you like my feathers, ladies use them to decorate their hats because I am like no other?" Ruth reached out and stoked the creature and found the feathers very soft and long. Emu turned her head and plucked out a feather and offered it to Ruth. "A token, to remember our meeting! May I have one of your feathers?" Ruth cautiously lowered her head, closed her eyes and waited for Emu to tug her hair but she didn't feel a thing. Emu turned and sauntered back to the watering hole to join her mate and quench her thirst.

"Thank you, Emu." Ruth called out.

In the meantime Liam felt a strange energy invading his space and nervously turned to find a large red kangaroo towering over him. "Hello mate, I am Boomer." He announced in a deep baritone voice. "This is my habitat, my family and I roam these plains by night and rest by day. Mrs Boomer is busy caring for our Joey who is safe in her pouch, so I thought I should come and introduce myself."

Liam felt quite intimidated as the large shadow covered his eyes from the sun. He noted the huge hind legs that allowed Boomer to bounce across the plain and the long rudder of a tail that helped propel the creature.

"If I went to the Olympic Games, I bet I would win a gold medal for the long jump." Boomer announced proudly throwing out his chest and beating it with his front paws.

While Liam was engrossed with Boomer, Isobel had noticed a small creature propped beside Boomer who was trying to get her attention, she knelt down and reached out her hand in friendship, "Hello who are you?"

"I am Frilly Lizard, we have roamed this land for thousands of years, and I am one of the ancient Ones." He announced proudly in a gruff voice. "Many of my ancestors left this planet, eons ago. Do you want to see what I do to protect myself? Look at this; it makes me appear much bigger than I am."

Immediately he stood on his hind legs, puffed up his cheeks and a magnificent green frill appeared around his neck.

"That is so clever and you look extremely beautiful when you wear your finery like that," cooed Isobel amazed at how such a delicate creature could camouflage himself.

"And that's not all I can do. It was very nice to meet you Isobel." Frilly lizard turned and raced back to the watering hole to show Isobel how fast he could run.

Tamara and Alistar had become distracted by a litter of pups who bounced in and out of the tall grasses playing hide-and-seek, while their Mother watched over them. "Your children are very boisterous it must be a full time job keeping track of six little people?" Tamara inquired of Mrs Dingo who sat watchful.

"Yes they are adorable while they are this age but in a few months time they will be able to leave the nest and travel out into the desert. Our breed does not always stay in packs some of us are loners, especially the males."

The puppies stopped play and lifted their heads to investigate the strangers scent and Tamara could hear the soft growls coming from their throats, as the puppies moved closer crawling on their bellies. Mrs Dingo lifted her head and barked an okay signal to her brood and they came running to great the visitors.

Just as the friends were walking to join Tamara and Alistar the hologram changed scene and they found themselves in the Rainforest beside a deep pond surrounded by large rocks.

"That was a quick change. It's hard to keep up with this journey. I wonder where we are now." Petra peered through the vegetation trying to get her bearings and the others stood quite still observing the magnificent fauna. Tall tree ferns created a canopy which protected a vast selection of undiscovered, native species which adorned the forest floor.

"Well we must be here for a good reason, lets take a look around." Liam offered. "Mind where you tread these rocks may be slippery." "Did you see that?" Jacob thought he saw a flash of movement in the water but wasn't sure if it had been an illusion. He squatted down to get a clearer view and the others joined him. After a few moments a large black bill broke the surface of the water, two small eyes were watching them, watching it.

"Who are you friend?" asked Joel gently trying not to frighten the water creature. "We have come to meet with the Australian creatures because we are all going to take a journey there in the near future." But the creature had disappeared again. "Have you seen a creature like that before?" Joel questioned his friends with a puzzled look on his face.

"NO," They replied in unison, "Never." So they waited patiently. At the same time they were totally unaware that they too were being watched and were startled when a voice spoke to them from behind a massive bush of maiden hair.

"Hello, have you lost something?" Wombat inquired in a squeaky voice as he wobbled towards the group. "If you are curious about my friend, he is a Platypus and this is his native environment. Not many folks get the pleasure of meeting platypus because they live under the water and build their nest there, to raise the pups. Very playful! But unfortunately not many can be found these days, they are protected by Conservation laws." Wombat informed them in a matter of fact way.

"Oh you made us jump! We didn't know you were there." Squealed Esha clutching her chest and quickly standing up to survey where the voice had come from. "Who are you?"

The friends turned around but remained seated on the rocks waiting for an explanation from the round, brown furry creature, while his small eyes inspected them. Wombat moved closer to Esha and sat down beside her.

"I am Wombat and I live here. Many of the creatures in this forest are marsupials and they have retired for the day. So you will not get the pleasure of meeting them, so I came as their representative to welcome you to our home. And as I have already explained platypus is a very shy creature. He may not show his face again."

Wombat turned and beckoned to an unseen friend and a small pointed nose peeped around the tree trunk, "Come on out, it's okay." And he waited for Echidna to join them. "This is my friend Echidna he eats ants and grubs on the forest floor. Please don't touch him because he will leave quills in your hand and they are very painful to humans and other animals. That's how he protects himself. Even I do not get to close to him. But he is my friend."

"Thank you for the introduction and your information, we are most pleased to make your acquaintance and feel very privileged to have visited your home." Liam acknowledged holding out his hand.

Within a flash the hologram changed again and the friends found themselves sitting on a high outcrop of rocks. Standing proudly before them, an aboriginal Warrior with a long spear pointing to the sky, his body adorned with white ochre paint, his ebony skin shone like silk in the brilliant sunlight. A large Goanna propped by his side. The band of friends quickly rallied to their feet wondering if their lives were being threatened and if they should speak, collectively they remained silent.

"We are the Watchers and Keepers of this Ancient land. If you follow me I will show you the story of our people. Inside this cave behind you on the walls are the drawings from long ago, put here by my ancestors to remind us of our beginnings. This time capsule has not been discovered by white man because these are our Sacred Sites, our records of the Dream Time. Please follow me." The warrior spoke quietly to goanna and asked him to keep watch outside the Cave entrance.

"We have decided to give you the privilege of '*Knowing*' our distant past because you have bravely volunteered to come to this land on your next journey." The warrior talked them through the story that was written in art form on the rock face and half an hour later led them back into the sunshine. "We will meet again dear friends. Farewell."

The skies were clear blue and the Sun at its zenith, a bright light flashed before their eyes and they found themselves back in the garden surrounded by familiar grounds. And yet it appeared that no time had passed.

"We better go back to see Nexus, he will be waiting for us."

∗ ∗ ∗ ∗ ∗

Nexus stood at the door with a welcome, "Did you enjoy my little surprise?" His big smile was hidden under the long white beard but his eyes were shining. "Just a quick meander through a land you will come to know. Sit down everybody, not much more to say now but there are words of wisdom and some insights I would like to share with you."

"We had a great time meeting all those unusual animals and especially when we were shown those amazing rock art stories of long ago." Jacob replied.

"Can those creatures be found in other parts of the world?" Ruth was curious to know.

"No they cannot. I wanted you to have recall of the land you are going too because there will be enough surprises waiting for you when you get there." Nexus tried to break the news gently and he wanted to put them on notice that this coming life would be very different than any previous life with pluses and minuses.

Nexus waited patiently for everyone to settle and bring their attention back to his studio.

"From time to time (we) the Masters will seed your fertile minds with new upgraded ideas and advanced inventions for the greater good of Mankind.

I am sharing this, so you will feel secure that we have your best intentions in mind. And that you will not be left to work out the complexities without guidance. You have bravely stepped forward for this mission and we salute your dedication to this genesis, a world that still has far to go to reach its true potential. And yet all is timely, my friends." He reached out and touched each person on the head for reassurance.

"We will open the 'Ideas Factory door' from time to time when appropriate to protect your valuable natural resources and the planet. The answers to your major problems will all be scribed but I fear the Dark Overlords will wish to remain in control to rule by fear and scarcity, thus refusing to go forward with this registered information." For a brief moment a dark shadow crossed his face.

"So you are telling us to….." Jacob couldn't quite get his mind around the information.

"Don't fall into the trap of fear or manipulation of commercial funds and goods. There is sufficient for everyone. Live a simple life. Do not clutter your personal world. Ask only for your needs not your wants; otherwise you may get caught up with the exploitation of the *money lenders* and *multinationals* greed. Walk with the trees, grow your own sustenance and drink fresh water. Meditate on solutions to your personal problems for you already carry the answers within. Believe in yourself and your journey. Share your knowledge with like-minded folks and support one another." Nexus paused and looked into the distance.

"I see that you will all travel from your birth land to bring a new light to a far away country that is ancient yet not fully established. A land that is surrounded by sea and quite removed from the old energy influences of previous empires. A young land in the making! Here you can create a new matrix by collecting the good from each past civilisation and build a new world of equality."

The friends sat and listened intently, although the information didn't seem to make sense to them right now.

"The pen will always be Mightier than the Sword. The prophesies I wrote, so long ago will be available for you to read which by now have been translated into many languages and when you do, you will remember this day." Once more Nexus walked around the room with his has clasped behind his back contemplating his next words of encouragement.

"The female gender is more attuned to crystal energies and will become assistants in the practice of delivering their cosmic rays. While the male gender, is more likely to be connected with the extraction of minerals from the earth. That is why we speak to you all as a collective of these coming events. You will each play an important role to safe guard the land, the oceans and the precious waterways."

"So what are you saying is that we will become conversationalist? Won't we have enough to do? It seems the list gets longer and longer." Joel stated feeling disheartened.

"And how are we supposed to fit all this into one life time?" Petra was starting to feel uncomfortable about the journey. There seemed so much to achieve.

"It all sounded fairly simple at the beginning of the day, now I'm not so sure." Ruth sighed to herself.

Tyler stood up and approached Nexus, "Are you sure we can accomplish all that you have spoken of? We were so full of excitement to think we would be travelling together on this journey, I guess it was your job to give us a reality check. But I can see why, this is a mission about *service* and we must not get caught up in our personal affairs?" Pause. "Am I right Nexus..... I can see by the look on your face that I have hit the nail on the head." Tyler turned to face his friends, "We need to centre ourselves before we leave this room and change our attitude about 180 degrees or we will fail completely."

"You are right Tyler we became caught up in the moment. Okay everybody join hands and we will focus on the job at hand. We have been instructed with extra insights and for this we thank you Nexus and Hathor for sparing us your precious time. Let's just be quiet for a few moments." Alistar instructed his friends. The band of friends closed their eyes and sat in silence and each remembered why they had volunteered for this coming mission.

Nexus broke the silence, "Now I only have a few more words of wisdom for you, each one of you have been given three special gifts. They are spiritual gifts of *knowingness* which will guide you all your life. Be prudent and watchful. And I will connect with you again when you return. Safe journey!" Nexus ushered them out the door and returned to his new invention, whistling a soft tune to himself.

Once outside the building the friends looked at each other, "So what do we do now?"

"Let's go down to that Coffee Lounge amongst the trees, it's not far from here because I would like a nice hot cup of chocolate. That is always great for my taste buds." Esha suggested, smiling in anticipation.

"That's a excellent idea, we can sit and have a chat about any reservations we might have. Are you all sure about this journey now we have some extra information?" Ruth inquired.

"Well now you come to mention it, I still have a few questions." Liam braved the moment to voice his thoughts and niggling doubts.

15 QUESTIONS

Why don't we remember when we are on Earth?
Because that's what we do!

"You know what I dislike most?" questioned Liam. "When we first arrive on Earth and come out of that dark tunnel into the bright lights, the nurses take us away from our Mothers just when we need comforting the most. Then they shut us up in a nursery with a whole lot of newcomers who are crying for the same reason. We are alone again. It's an awful feeling, as if it wasn't hard enough getting out of that small space in the first place."

"And what else upsets the poor little boy?" teased Ruth pulling a face at him.

"It's not funny you know." Liam was trying to have a serious moan. "Those first two years are so frustrating."

"Oh it's easier being a girl we don't fight that feeling so much. I just try and sleep away that time so it will go quickly." Esha purred, smiling at Liam.

"At least as an Asian child I will be strapped to my Mother and I will be able to hear her regular heart beat."

"Well that won't happen for me, I'll be left parked in the corner of the kitchen inhaling all those cooking smells. That is a great distraction from sleeping." Liam moaned.

"Can you hear yourselves? We haven't even left this place yet. Are you sure you want to go? It's not too late to retract your enrolment form." Ruth became agitated and spoke her mind. "We are supposed to be enjoying this time together."

"Yes, but it's." Jacob started to stand up for Liam but Ruth cut him off.

"That's enough. If we all start focusing on those new beginnings none of us will step up to be counted."

"Well you must admit the first two years are difficult, just trying to communicate what it is that you want. Parents have to guess half the time." Joel quickly intervened before Ruth could put up her hand in a gesture of peace.

"And getting our bodies to do what we want them too do is horrendous. I can never pick up what I'm aiming for or it slips through my fingers." Tyler replied.

Tamara had been sitting quietly listening to all the rhetoric, smiling to herself. "Well it appears you boys have all the trouble adjusting. Why don't you just surrender to the conditions and enjoy the nurturing while it lasts? When you become adults you might allow your partners to nurture your relationships instead of being in control of every situation. You don't have to be MR

Macho you know. You are allowed to express your feelings without frustration. We will be there for you, remember."

"Yes this is a new time frame when life will be different. All time frames are different. And if we are to be the teachers we have to set an example." Alistar reminded them.

"Okay I've had my whinge and got that off my chest. I agree we must leave here with a positive outlook or we will take the negative thoughts with us. Thank you for bringing me back on track." Liam hung his head in shame and reached out to Petra for assurance.

"You will be fine. We all have to pass through these stages of growth and learning, it's amazing that we all keep going back for more, especially as we know what it will be like mastering the physical body. We will all be fine just you wait and see." Petra patted his hand, then bought it to her lips and kissed it gently.

"But I just wish we could remember this place when we are in Earth consciousness." Liam's face was full of unanswered questions as he pondered his statement.

"Well you heard what the Masters promised that this time we could have access to our Soul computer and learn to communicate with them through new techniques. That's very reassuring to me." Alistar tried to commiserate. "Cheer up."

"And the Masters have promised to guide our footsteps, every step of the journey."

"There is always a celebration when we leave this place, we have just experienced that and coming together like this is so reassuring before we take our next steps. Don't you agree?" Isobel pipped up so they would take the focus of parting. "And when we return there will be another celebration to welcome us back for a job well done. Each way we burst through the tunnel of darkness and arrive in a pool of Light, whether we are coming or going. Anyway how do you tell whether we are coming or going? It's just a circle!"

Jacob agreed, "And there is always *family* waiting to greet us. That's the good part. At least they are not strangers who have never known us before. This side of the veil there are the Masters and on Earth, there are our parents. Not so bad after all."

"So has anyone else got something to say?" Esha smiled as their energy lifted.

"This was a great idea Esha. This chocolate is famous but the chocolate on Earth is divine, I remember now, we didn't have it very often but when we did, what a treat!" Jacob grinned over the top of his cup.

"Are you going to have some pets in this lifetime," Tamara asked out of the blue.

"Whatever made you think of that?" Tyler asked surprised at the question.

"When I read the brochure some of those house pets sounded so nice. Cats, dogs and tropical fish or maybe a goat? It's good for children to grow up with pets, it teaches them to be responsible for other creatures and they learn about life and death in a different way. Its more, gentle. And they can grow emotionally and share their love with someone else. These are great learning curves for children and very comforting in times of uncertainty." Ruth explained the psychology.

"I don't think I ever had a pet. Most of my lifetimes we have had many animals but they were always for eating, riding or protecting our village." Joel commented out loud.

"I remember the beautiful temple cats, sleek and slender with amazing blue eyes their duty was to guard the high walls surrounding the Temple. They could almost talk to you but we couldn't have them as pets." Petra reminisced.

"Well if we are going to live in Australia we will all have to learn to swim?" Alistar decided to change the subject. He would think about pets much later.

"Why?"

"Because, in the future we will spend lots of time on those gorgeous beaches. There will be plenty of sunshine and blue seas! Most of the population live close to the coast and swimming is their recreation, apart from the fact that it can get very hot. The best way to finish a day, have a swim." Alistar explained and on a more serious note, "And I don't want anyone to drown and find themselves back here to soon. We all have to complete this mission and meet up as we planned."

"Okay then, we will all learn to swim." Everyone agreed and nodded their heads.

"Well, I'm going to have lots of pets." Isobel announced.

"Good for you."

"On a more important note, has anyone visited their earth mother? The blessed ones, who at this moment carry our new physical bodies," Ruth offered a new thought. "There's no one else present, I had a quick scan and there isn't anyone to interrupt us, so I suggest we sit quietly in a circle and take time out from our worries and make a quick trip to connect with our new biology. Also, it will be comforting to feel the energy of our new Mothers. We have always done this in the past but we have been so caught up in the mission with our own questions and insecurities, I suggest that we had better reassure her that all is okay."

"Good idea," Tamara agreed. "We'll do that now. Is everybody ready?"

"Yes, that is a good idea! We don't need any mishaps at this late stage because we all want to be reassured that we will be arriving together."

The friends sat in silence and teleported their thoughts to their new future beginnings and each felt the love that was being sent to the forming child within. They heard their Mothers voice and responded to the sound waves.

They felt safe and warm within the cave of creation. Ten minutes later their consciousness returned to the present surroundings.

"That was great but it is getting a little cramped for space and I don't like lying there with my head pointing downwards." Liam stated when their attention was bought back to their present location.

"Don't be silly, Liam that's because there is not a lot of time left before we take that journey down the dark passage into the

Light." Isobel informed him, placing a gentle kiss on his cheek. "You will be fine."

"You mean it's all going to happen really soon?" Liam started to feel unsure about the situation. "So how much time do we have together?"

"I don't know but we sure have had fun during this last 24 hours. Look at what we have experienced and been shown to guide us. We all knew it would come to an end soon than later." Isobel tried to be rational and suggested they make tracks to investigate the next step in the process. "There must be a bulletin somewhere."

"Maybe it is on the brochure in our room? And we got caught in the energy of finding one another and we forgot to read the last paragraph." Joel spoke out loud while scanning his memory banks for a clue.

16
HOT CHOCOLATE

Suddenly a loud gong resonated around the complex and bought them to attention. ***"Will all registered participates for the Rescue Mission please assemble, in the tall White Marble building and prepare for delivery."***

"But I'm not ready." Liam squeaked, almost having a panic attack while choking on his hot chocolate.

"Of course you are." Petra reached over and touched his hand. "If we just sit here being comfortable with each other, we will never move forward and take another journey and I am extremely excited about our next lifetime together. Liam I have loved you forever."

"I thought we would go back to our planet and take our leave of passage from there." Joel explained looking hopefully into their faces, waiting for conformation.

"Well we don't have to return to our planet or our sleeping quarters to find the information? Because we have now been given our final instructions?"

Isobel tried to ease the tension. She turned to look at Tyler and noticed his thoughts were far away. "Tyler you have been very quiet is anything the matter?"

"No. I still have a picture of my new Mother in my head and she looked so beautiful and radiant. She was in the garden on her hands and knees weeding the flower beds, humming to herself. The Sun was so warm on her skin, I could feel it."

"Well you are lucky, my Mother was rugged up sitting by an open fire because it was snowing outside," Joel offered. "And she was busy knitting some baby clothes. But I could feel she was anxious, there was a lot of loud noise outside the house and I think she was waiting for my father to come home. I could smell something delicious cooking in the kitchen. I guess that's a good sign that she's a great cook. I hope she knows how to make hot chocolate like this."

Ruth butted in, "I think this is a good conclusion because we only have to say goodbye to each other, once. If we had to return to our planets, we would have to do that twice and at least we are all here together."

"That's true." They all agreed. "Let's look on the bright side."

The hot chocolate started to take effect, tickling their endorphins and their mood lifted.

"I saw my Mother too she wears the most beautiful gowns. She was choosing an evening dress from her wardrobe to attend an opening night Fashion Parade and my Father sat watching her. He was so proud of his talented wife. He walked over and caressed her blooming belly with such tenderness I could feel his love passing through her body." Petra shared her experience joyfully. "How about you Jacob, how did you feel about your Mother? Is she nice too?"

"It was quite different for me, my Mother was kneeing before Buddha in a huge temple giving thanks for conceiving her first child. I could smell incense and feel humility. I think she had been trying to have a child for some time." A wide smile lite up Jacobs face as he continued. "She's a very gentle soul but there is an inner strength about her beyond her years. Esha how did you find your Mother, was she nice too?"

"My new Mother is a great cook too because her parents own a restaurant but she is a very busy lady at the moment and working long hours. I felt it was time for her to put her feet up and rest a bit more. She has a happy smile and beautiful dark eyes. I think she felt my presence because she quickly sat down and put her hands on her belly then took some deep breathes. Maybe I needed to remind her to slow down and rest a little because her time was near. I need her to conserve some of her energy."

"Just look at that amazing sunset." The band of friends all turned to witness the array of luminous colours painted across the pink sky. Time had slipped away from them as they shared the good news of their future parents.

"We will have to make tracks very soon." Ruth announced with a soulful voice. "But we haven't heard about Alistar and Tamara's parents. I'm sure we won't be missed yet, there are so many others who can go first." She turned and waited for Alistar to reply.

"My grandparents were one of the early settlers who came from Ireland and went to Kalgoorlie during the Gold rush, they lived in a tent and my mother was born during hard times when rations were simple. It was not any easy life but my grandfather was a lucky one he discovered a very fruitful vein on his plot of land and made a lot of money. Now he owns some of the best property in town. My mother married into a wealthy family. Although she is a plain looking woman with a very gentle disposition and a loving heart, I know she is strong and well balanced in her outlook on life." Then he looked at Ruth and reminded her that she had not offered her findings of her mother. "Tell us Ruth, come on."

"Well it was a bit sad, my parents were at the London Underground Railway saying their goodbyes because my Father is about to leave England and to go France to join the French Resistance. It had all been very secret and they only found out about his departure a few days before. There were many tears. But his last goodbye was to the child she was carrying. He promised to write as soon as he could get a letter to her." Ruth conveyed in a forlorn voice trying to hold back her own tears.

"Oh! Ruth, that is so sad for you. I am sure you will be a great comfort to your Mother." Esha tried to console her friend and tried to shed some positive thoughts on the matter. "Well your Mum won't have long to wait, you will soon be in her arms. In these times one never knows what war will bring and everyone lives life for the moment, I'm sure she is happy that their love conceived a child. You will bring her so much joy."

"What can I say, we all choose our parents to fit the journey we were about to take and we know what troublesome times we are about to enter. I will just have to stay strong for the both of us and fill her world with love." Ruth announced in a matter of fact tone. "I can do that, I know I can."

Suddenly, Joel felt uncomfortable with Ruth's news and decided that time was moving on, "We can't sit here chatting like this; the 'Call' has already been given for us to go."

"But we haven't heard about Tamara's mother. Come on Tamara we still have time to hear about your Mother." Alistar reached out and held her hands in his and looked deep into her eyes. "Joel you will have to be patient for a little bit longer."

"My mother works in a suburban Deli and lives upstairs, her husband is a chauffer for a very important Member of Parliament, so he is away sometimes for many days. During the evenings she goes to help assemble munitions at the factory. As you can imagine, she must be an extremely organised person. And she wants lots of children. I am sure I will learn many skills from her that will assist me in my lifetime." Tamara reported. "She is a matter of fact kind of lady and holds her emotions to herself but I know that when I arrive she will feel the love inside her and it will overflow, bringing her much joy." Alistar gave Tamara a big hug, while everyone waited for them to finish their embrace.

"So can we go now?" Joel inquired. He had become fidgety and impatient and a bit apprehensive about the eminent goodbyes.

17
BIRTHING CHAMBER

The Coffee Lounge had been situated in a secluded part of the large gardens, away from the hustle and bustle of the enormous crowds and as they emerged from the shaded area the noise stopped them in their tracks.   Excitement filled the air as hundreds of volunteers walked expectantly towards the White Marble building that had a thousand golden candles shining from its windows. The long winding pathway was scattered with glowing crystals and precious gems which acted as a sedative to the soul.   While the aura of lights appeared like a veil of welcome and created a festive atmosphere drawing the crowd gently towards the building like a magnet. One by one they passed through the glass doorway and disappeared across the rose quartz hallway to the birthing chamber.

"That is the most beautiful building I have ever seen. Can you feel the overwhelming love that is emanating from there?" Esha wanted to stand still and just look at the architecture but found herself moving forward, drawn by the energy.

"It reminds me of a huge, three tier wedding cake except it has lots of windows. Do you think they are really windows?" Ruth was looking up, her mouth open in wonder. Joel walked close beside her, their hands entwined, enjoying the physical connection as they came closer to the moment of separation. "Each step we take we get closer to connecting again. Joel, I will carry this moment in my heart until I see you again. It's very exciting, don't you think?" Ruth turned and found Joel with shinning eyes and a wide smile. The apprehension had subsided as the sweet energy of the crystal engulfed them.

Tyler whispered in Isobel's ear, "We are going to have a wonderful life together this time. I keep seeing those beautiful beaches in Australia. And those amazing animals we met."

"Doesn't it sound great but we will also have other novel opportunities to learn new techniques which we will share with those not so fortunate, those who don't have the knowledge. Now that's very exciting." Isobel enjoyed being a teacher and had worked with children many lifetimes. Watching them discover the joy of reading and writing made her heart sing.

Esha and Jacob were the first to arrive at the entrance. A shower of bright light covered them as they passed through the doorway, washing away the memories of the past 24 hours. An Angel guided them to the crystal staircase and motioned for them to ascend. Their friends quickly followed behind. The staircase moved gently upwards which gave them a feeling of buoyantancy and carried them to the second floor. Many others followed behind them and when they looked back there was a continuous stream of volunteers.

"I wonder, what happens on the first floor?" Liam queried looking downwards.

"Well I can only guess it's for those who haven't yet mastered the physical and emotional conditions of being human. Maybe it's for those who have yet to complete their karmic ties or young souls taking their first journey into third density." Alistar offered tactfully.

"You are probably right. I hadn't thought about that but it makes sense." Liam agreed turning to observe their progress. "We are nearly there. I hope there are some instructions."

As they approached the second floor they stepped onto a Rose Quartz floor and at the central point stood a magnificent glass arbour which displayed a prolific collection of orchids from all around the galaxies. Their beauty and colours were breathtaking and a sweet scent filled the air.

"Have you ever seen such beautiful flowers?" Petra stood before the glass walls magically drawn to the display. "I didn't realise there were so many colours, shapes and sizes. Some of these specimens must be native plants which grow in the rainforest of tropical lands and of which man has never seen before in their natural state. Look at that one, it drapes like a bridal bouquet, tiny white clusters, so delicate. Just like a handful of little stars which have been scooped up and attached to a long stem."

"Oh I like this one! Soft pink petals with a deep maroon tongue with yellow spots. There must be at least twelve flowers on that one spike. And look how tall that spike is!" Tamara stared with wonder. "Which one do you prefer Esha?"

"This one, it's almost an emerald green and has a stripy effect on the upper petals. That one would be more difficult to find in its natural environment as the colour would be a great camouflage in the forest. I didn't know that there was a species that were green." Esha moved closer to the glass to inspect the depth of colour, until her nose pressed against it. "Some of those flowers are so small."

"Have you seen that beautiful specimen of Maiden hair fern standing on that gorgeous, carved pedestal in the centre of the display?" Ruth was fascinated by the sheer size of the plant growing in the ceramic container and how the fronds spilled gently over the edge.

They were so ingrossed in the display of orchids that they didn't hear the Golden Angel approaching them, to guide their footsteps.

"This way please." The Golden Angel announced. "Please follow me, dear ones."

"Oh you made me jump." Ruth reached out and grabbed Joel's hand and whispered, "Where are we going?"

"How would I know?" Joel whispered in reply.

In the meantime the others had coupled up also holding hands for reassurance, as the Golden Angel led them down a long corridor and then came to a stop in front of a large, Perspex door. "Please enter and change into your astrological colours. I will wait for your return and then we will move on."

As the band of friends entered the room, a glass cylinder descended from the ceiling which surrounded each one and with a soft hiss enfolded them with a delicate, translucent light which changed colours according to the astrological year of their forthcoming birth. This procedure took only a few seconds to complete and within no time the gang found themselves filing back out the door. The Golden Angel waited to guide them to the next event.

"Masters you look most beautiful in your radiant colours. Congratulations! We will now proceed to the Birthing Chamber. Many Ascended Masters are preparing, to be you. Please follow me." The Golden Angel bowed, in respect and a smile crossed his serene face with joy and divine love. Joy that he, could be of service to these brave souls who were about to venture forward with an awesome mission. To carry Light and Love into a world that appeared to have been engulfed with a Dark cloud of disharmony. The Golden Angel continued down the long passageway, the band of friends followed close behind until they reached another large door which opened as they approached. Before he ushered them forward he whispered, "Farewell, dear Ones. One day in the future we will meet again."

Soft music welcomed them into a circular room adorned with white, chiffon flowing curtains and rose petals covered the floor. Another Angel guided them to the centre of the room, "Please sit in a circle on the floor and hold hands. You have a few minutes to centre yourselves while you sit in meditation." There was no more time for personal communication between the friends, they quietly responded to the instructions.

The door opened and the twelve Ascended Masters filed into the room and stood in a circle behind the ones waiting to be birthed. And then a band of Angels entered the room and filed in and stood behind the Ascended Masters.

"We have decided that you may leave this place together. We see the love bond that binds you and we honour your dedication to this mission. Remember you are truly loved and that we will guide your footsteps until you return to us. On that day we will be here to welcome you and listen to your story. You are Blessed and Divine beings from our Creator."

The choir of Angels raised gentle voices in salutations and farewell. Within a few minutes there came a white flash of brilliant light and the small circle of friends had begun their new journey.

"HERE WE GO, HERE WE GO!"
CONGRATULTIONS
CONCLUSION

There are a select few, Mentors, who have gone before you, to prepare and guide your footsteps. In time you will come to recognise the part they played in your life. WE call them the 'Devoted Ones'. Remember you are never alone. There will be those who return to US who will still continue to guide your footsteps and love you through your journey.

There will be many conspiracy theories that will need to be exposed, for the truth has been hidden by those who control the world through finances and religion. Look for the signposts.

NOTES

Brochure (please **read** the small print)

Things to delight the senses - smells, sights, and hearing

Tools to take with you

Things they don't tell you

No Instruction Manual when you get there

NO map.   You are here!

On holiday, Ha! Ha! Get lost, become sick, loose money / possessions and baggage

No replacement parts – must 'Self heal'

NO return ticket for 75 years

Small print – Not refundable / not transferable

One way ticket - traffic jam, lose spiritual family

One way ticket - how do I get home?

Price of return ticket - Complete your mission.

MORALE of story - beware of B.B.Q's or don't make plans when your Intoxicated with Celestial Cider - made from apples. Beware of bubbles

Ethereal Eggnog	Bloody Mary	Jolly Joseph
Beloved Beer	Radiant Rum	Angelic Aniseed
Galactic Gin / Tonic		

DO'S	DON'TS
Remain an individual	Become a sheep
Mix with nature / wildlife	Live in concrete jungle
Smile	Frown
Have fun	Be too serious
Create	Destroy
Survive	Surrender

Next Light Ship 1000 years before due on Planet Earth – wait for cancellation

Transmit ion from the Galactic Council

"Beloved Earth Angels you have completed your contract to prevent Armageddon.

You have changed the world forever and now it can continue on the road to recovery.

Congratulations."

1999

"Beloved Earth Angels you have now achieved critical mass and the Consciousness

of the world can move forward into more Peaceful Times but first the negative energies

must be transmuted into the positive.

2002

PEACEMAKERS 2 –	Living In Duality
	Arseholes and Angels
PEACEMAKERS 3 –	Transformation
	Karma Waters